The Failure of Success

Redefining what matters

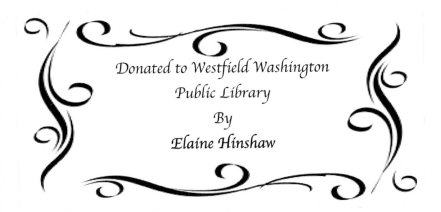

The Failure
of Success

Redefining what matters

Jennifer Kavanagh

BOOKS

Winchester, UK
Washington, USA

First published by O-Books, 2012
O-Books is an imprint of John Hunt Publishing Ltd., Laurel House, Station Approach,
Alresford, Hants, SO24 9JH, UK
office1@o-books.net
www.o-books.com

For distributor details and how to order please visit the 'Ordering' section on our website.

ISBN: 978 1 78099 765 0

A CIP catalogue record for this book is available from the British Library.

Design: Stuart Davies

Printed in the USA by Edwards Brothers Malloy

We operate a distinctive and ethical publishing philosophy in all
areas of our business, from our global network of authors to
production and worldwide distribution.

CONTENTS

By the same author
The Methuen Book of Animal Tales (ed.)
The Methuen Book of Humorous Stories (ed.)
Call of the Bell Bird
The World is our Cloister
New Light (ed.)
Journey Home (formerly The O of Home)
Simplicity Made Easy
Small Change, Big Deal

If you can meet with triumph and disaster
And treat those two impostors just the same...
Rudyard Kipling, "If"

In writing this book, I have talked to a wide variety of people: people I know; people I've met; some that I have deliberately sought out. I have talked to a teenager, a woman in her eighties and others in all the decades in between. I wanted to know about perceptions of success and failure in education, in business, public life, and in the voluntary sector. I wanted to hear from entertainers, poets, and priests; meet those whose work is to evaluate success, and those for whom the concept doesn't exist. Some names have been changed. To all, profound thanks.

References in the text are to books listed in Further reading. When there is more than one work by the same author, they are distinguished in textual references by their date of publication.

References to the Bible
KJV = King James Version
NIV = New International Version

The success culture

Success! What a glorious, ringing, resounding sound that has. Something golden to reach out for, a pinnacle to attain. Passing, winning, beating – success is heady stuff. We all have images in our mind: of applause, champagne, triumphant smiles, curtain calls, laps of honour, and of parading through cities in open-top buses.

Actually, according to the Oxford English Dictionary, the original meaning of success was an outcome, whether good or bad: just something that follows. This meaning is still in use in the word "succession" when one person follows or "succeeds" another in a role or in a family. The current usage of the word "success", however, shows a shift to "the prosperous achievement of something attempted; the attainment of an object according to one's desire, now with particular reference to the attainment of wealth or position".

This concept of success (and its frightening shadow, failure) is embedded in our culture.

Given the magnitude of its profile, the enduring attraction of books on how to attain success in every aspect of our lives, from the seminal *How to Succeed at Business without really trying* onwards, comes as no surprise. We devour advice on how to succeed with women, at interviews, golf, work and even at breastfeeding. There is no part of our lives, it seems, in which we ought not to be striving for success. Not succeeding, failure to succeed, is a humiliation beyond bearing.

It is common for high achievers in many different areas to say, as the athlete, Kelly Holmes, has done, "You can do anything you want to if you set your mind to it." This is an understandably popular attitude when applied to triumphing over adversity. We all like to be encouraged, to feel that we can make it, even in difficult circumstances. One story that hits all the right notes is that of George Walker, a Billingsgate porter from the East End of London, who became a successful boxer. When injury forced him to retire from the ring, he went into business, and built a huge empire, including Brent Cross, one of the early London shopping malls. As his obituary said, "He went on to buy hundreds of pubs, a chain of casinos, the Brighton Marina and the William Hill betting shops" (the *Independent*, 26 March, 2011). What it didn't say is that he was also made bankrupt in the early 90s, and charged with – and acquitted of – theft by the Serious Fraud office.

Success in one aspect of life can pull the rest of life out of balance, often causing a high level of stress and even illness. The *Independent* reported that "as befits someone who has been alternately idolised and demonised by the press, [Mike] Tyson is wary of the public's continuing interest in his saga. He says that celebrity made him 'delusional' and that it has taken nothing less than a 'paradigm shift' for him to come down to earth. 'We have to stick to what we are. I always stay in my slot. I know my place.'"

It also has a considerable impact on the family. Those who have achieved extreme success in their work or calling are often even more out of balance, and often notoriously unsuccessful in personal relationships. Consider the personal lives of, for instance, Marilyn Monroe, Gandhi or Beethoven. Intense focus excludes other parts of life, as if there simply isn't enough energy to support relationships as well as a career or creative gift. Sometimes it is easier to give our attention to external "doing" than to the complex and problematic state of being in relationship.

Success, of course, often has a public dimension, attracting praise and bestowing status. Some people are famous merely for being famous, but generally fame is as a result of perceived success in a publicly observable field. Above all, to be successful implies wealth and influence – and a high place in a hierarchy. The cult of celebrity has infiltrated every aspect of public life, from politics to artistic performance, and exerts considerable pressure on those in its spotlight. It is no longer enough to be a fine writer, a virtuoso violinist, or someone who knows everything about taxation. People have to be media-savvy, promotable, celebrity-worthy – if possible, glamorous. Above all, visibly successful.

Public success goes beyond an individual or team achievement: everyone wants a bit of it. Unconnected others claim an association with those achieving success: "our" football team, a tennis player from our country, autograph-seeking fans, each hoping that by touching success some of it will rub off. The private lives of those in the public eye absorb millions of other people in a vicarious and voyeuristic way: even much of our "news" revolves round events in the lives of a few high-profile individuals. Celebrity seems to tell us that we are of worth only if we are noticed. We want what they have, and reality TV makes it all too easy to believe that a bit of talent can bring quick-fix success without too much effort.

In my local café, Rob acknowledges our dependence on celebrities. He gestures towards the show playing on the TV up in the corner of the room: "We're indoctrinated to get our happiness through them. Sad, really." Success is glossier than achievement or just being good at something. It has a public sheen, expects awards, presentations and public recognition. And it takes its toll.

Visible success, or fame, is particularly stressful. Richard Olivier, son of two renowned actors, talked of the impact of public attention on his parents and on himself as a child. Constant media attention is hard to live with: privacy is difficult to maintain. Even at times of family crises, doorstepping photographers try to capture a moment to publish to the world. Fame, Oliver feels, is powerful – and dangerous. People either can't deal with it – some taking to drink or drugs – or they believe in the inflated public image of themselves, and come to believe they can do no wrong. When it ends, and the applause stops, adjustment to "normal" life is hard. We have seen many examples among politicians and other people in the public eye. Sportsmen such as footballers can be particularly vulnerable. Huge success and wealth can come very young; the career is short-lived; and plans are not always in place for a life afterwards, a life perhaps from as young as 35 onwards when a former star has to adjust to a life without public acclaim. One former Indian cricketer talked of the adulation and the pressure of an existence as an international player: "If you do well, they treat you like gods. You earn huge sums of money. It's hard to let it go." The pop singer Adam Ant, talking of life before and after a mental breakdown, said of the pressure of his huge success: "No one can prepare you for that."

Children of successful people often struggle with their own lives, especially if their parents' success has drawn public attention to their children, if busy parents have neglected them, or similarly high standards are expected. Even if parents' expectations are not excessive, the role modelled for the children can be daunting; their own expectations may be unrealistic. Their talents may lie in fields quite different from those of their parents, and possibly less public.

It's hard to satisfy the need for success. Winning is often not enough. Winning all the championships in one year, winning more championships than anyone else, being the most capped player, taking the most wickets, making the most runs, selling the most records, being not only top of the bestseller list but staying there for longer than anyone else – in some, the need and greed for success can never be satisfied. The quest can become addictive. George Walker explained the addictive nature of financial success. "When I get into something new and it starts making money I look around for another place to do it. I'm like a squirrel on one of them barrels – the faster I run the faster the bloody thing goes." His motivation, he said, came from his background. "Anyone who has been poor must have the fear of going back. It stays with you all the time – the gut fear in any man has to be a spur."

* * *

Success in this model is based on a collection of stereotypes, including wealth, property, marriage, children, a circle of friends, and being respected in the local community. We may come to believe that we are judged by our house, our car, our job, even the holidays we take. The image of perfection created by an omnipresent edifice of advertising insists that success brings with it a certain body type exuding good health and fitness: the men sporty and tall, the women slim.

The result for many people is status anxiety. For anyone who doesn't fit the stereotype, be they gay, unable to have children, short, unfit, dyslexic or unemployed, it is not surprising that a sense of failure hovers. A South African friend put it more strongly: "Everything about you in magazines and so on shouts that you don't make the grade", leading to "a pervading sense of guilt and inadequacy" in society.

And we project our anxiety on to others, demonising particular groups, such as those in prison, people with mental health issues, and those of no fixed abode, labelling them losers and failures. Those stigmatised may well feel that their failure predated their current circumstances – indeed was likely to have been a contributory factor. Statistics show that those in prison are low in most of the indicators of "success", such as housing, education, employment, literacy, and relationships, before they went into prison – and often are lower still afterwards. Repeated failure leads to what psychologist Martin Seligman has called "learned helplessness", a condition in which the individual believes that he has no control over his life. "That is how it has always been, and nothing is going to change."

What we forget is that people falling into these groups are not some small minority. It is estimated that one in six of all people in the UK suffer from a significant mental health problem at any given time; that thousands of families live in temporary accommodation, and that at least 20% of the working population (and one in three men under 30) have criminal records. They are our neighbours. In other circumstances, they could be us. If we define success in material terms, then we are relegating not only these stigmatised groups to the abyss of failure, but much of the population. With a reference to the fact that the richest 1% in the United States own 1/3 of the net worth of that country, the rallying cry of the Occupy movements speaks for the rest of us:

We are the 99 percent. We are getting kicked out of our homes. We are forced to choose between groceries and rent. We are denied quality medical care. We are suffering from environmental pollution. We are working long hours for little pay and no rights, if we're working at all. We are getting nothing while the other 1 percent is getting everything. We are the 99 percent.

Ian, one of the founder-members of the Occupy London group, told me about a homeless man who had been sleeping outside St Paul's Cathedral for ten years. When the encampment joined him, he became part of a community, and his life was transformed. He was valued, he became part of the decision-making process, and he gave up drinking. "Why", asked Ian, "does Jim have so much value in our community, and none in the world outside? There is", he said, "a different currency at St Paul's."

A material-based definition of success discards most of humankind. Millions of people round the world are trapped in lives with few choices or opportunities to change them. Can we call that failure? In 1999 I went to Bangladesh, one of the poorest countries in the world. It was my first trip to a developing country and, before I went, I was asked if I was ready for the culture shock. I replied that I am easily upset but that I cannot for ever wear blinkers. In the event, I was amazed to discover that I was not upset, but moved by the courage, energy and dignity of those I met. As many others have testified, it was on re-entry to my own country that the culture shock kicked in. When the general standard of living is low, the struggle to surmount it is a communal one. It is making comparisons in an unequal society that lowers self-esteem, and leads to a sense of failure. Poverty is more shameful and oppressive in a generally wealthy culture.

It is in Britain that I have witnessed more of that "learned helpessness" – but, surprisingly, not generally among refugees, despite the fact that in many cases they have access to less help than those born here. Refugees have learnt to survive and have had the courage and energy to leave and start again. No, the helpessness is to be found more generally among those stuck in generations of unemployment and dependence on benefits. It is not one-off mistakes that do the damage, but the inability to recover – the "staying down". And it is our glittering success culture that helps to keep us there.

2

The nature of success

One secret of success in life is for a man to be ready for his opportunity when it comes. (Benjamin Disraeli)

However easy it is to be seduced by our celebrity culture into thinking of success in terms of wealth, prosperity and popularity, the successes of most of us tend to be modest affairs: a piano exam, a driving test, getting a job, buying a first flat, winning a tennis match or a race – meeting or surpassing our own and others' expectations.

Whether something feels like a success or a failure depends on the starting point. For all of us, every day is full of small achievements that we don't even notice. We think nothing of paying a bill – unless we have struggled to find the money, have problems with the system, or have been procrastinating. For a baby, to sit up or to take a first step is a huge achievement, a milestone. For someone with literacy problems, reading a page will feel like success. At different times of life, we will assess our actions in different ways. As we grow in competence in our chosen field we will think nothing of actions that years earlier would have felt like real achievements. As we age, reduced fitness may force us to reassess what we have taken for granted for most of our lives. For those with arthritic hips or knees, even going upstairs may feel like a success.

Expectation

Success does not stand on its own; it is only a level of achievement set against either a standard of expectation, or the achievements of others. And expectations are high. We are culturally conditioned to bring our children up to achieve: to attain success at school, in exams, and at work; to have a successful career. One of the women I talked to spoke for many in her description of early life as passing a series of tests: first the 11+, then "O" levels, "A" levels, and on to university. In the senior ranks of the civil service, she committed herself to climbing the ladder, even if the ladder was not something she really believed in.

Parental expectation (as we will see more fully in Chapter 6) plays a very significant part in our attitudes to success and failure, and helps to shape our own. Sometimes that expectation stems from a parent's sense of failure in their own lives, and their need for their children to succeed can exert a near intolerable pressure. It was striking to find that so many established people with independent lives were still striving to meet what they perceived as their parents' expectations, or retrospectively to win their approval. One young woman studies by day and works by night, and feels the need to achieve sporting success: from a triathlon to climbing Snowdon to cycling 2,000km for a charity. A woman from a Pakistani background said that her need to "collect trophies" in life was probably due to her strict upbringing. She had to go the *best* art school and then on to the *best* regiment in the army. Now that her parents are dead, and she has successfully evaded an arranged marriage, she is free to follow her own goals of writing a book and settling down to have children.

It is easy to take for granted our own cultural definitions. Teaching at an international school, where pupils represent about fifty different nationalities, gives a broader perspective. Sixteen years as head of admissions at the International School of London made Richard look critically at culture. When parents come to look round the school, they all say, "We're looking for a good school," but what that might mean, he says, is based mainly on their own schooling experience. Teachers at the school also come from many countries, and they don't necessarily agree about the criteria for success.

An extreme example of difference comes from Amy Chua, the Chinese American author of *Battle Hymn of the Tiger Mother*, who generalises her experiences as a Chinese parent:

> First, Chinese parents demand perfect grades because they believe that their child can get them. If their child doesn't get them, the Chinese parent assumes it's because the child didn't work hard enough. That's why the solution to substandard performance is always to excoriate, punish and shame the child. The Chinese parent believes that their child will be strong enough to take the shaming and to improve from it.
>
> Second, Chinese parents believe that their kids owe them everything...The understanding is that Chinese children must spend their lives repaying their parents by obeying them and making them proud.
>
> Third, Chinese parents believe that they know what is best for their children and therefore override all of their children's own desires and preferences. That's why Chinese daughters can't have boyfriends in high school and why Chinese kids can't go to sleepaway camp.

Nor are they allowed to be in a school play, watch TV or play computer games or choose their own extra-curricular activities. Getting any grade less than an A is unacceptable as is being less than the no. 1 student in every subject except gym and drama. They must play the piano or violin and no other instrument (*Wall St Journal*, 8 January 2011).

In our own culture, there are many different influences on our expectations, including social class. As the CEO of a charity told me: "Success breeds success. We're strongly bound by social class. I'm middle class, brought up with the expectation of success." Rob also feels that everything is just down to class. He spoke vehemently about external judgements – what paper you read, above all what you do. "Society judges you according to your job" – in his case, running a sandwich shop. "How you judge yourself deep down is another matter." In fact, as research into the "class ceiling"shows, there has been a flat-lining of social mobility over the past couple of decades. It has become harder to move beyond the social class we are born in. In education, in the working world, and in our very sense of ourselves, our level of expectation and what we actually achieve are too often set early in life.

Gender too is still an issue. Despite the progress that has been made in establishing equality in the workplace, breaking through glass ceilings is still a problem, not helped by some parental attitudes. Catherine said that she came from a sexist family, who wouldn't let her go to university, just wanting her to make a good marriage. After the birth of one girl, and the death of a baby boy, she felt that her own birth came as a disap-pointment to her parents, who were eventually mollified by the birth of her younger brother. She became bitter:

Marry a duke? I thought of men as the enemy. I left school at 15, had run away before. I needed to do something to prove that I was worthy to exist. I wanted to be better than my brother, and to do more and earn more, because that's what Dad thought was important.

Another woman referred to the "reflected glory" of her father's status as a vicar, and her husband's as a doctor, making it difficult for her (considerable) career to be recognised.

Others suffer from what Collette Dowling has called "The Cinderella Complex": a fear of independence, with an uncon-scious desire to be taken care of by others. Dowling describes her state during years of being at home with her children. "During all those years of a peculiar kind of Method acting known only to women, I hid from who I was." She quotes Alexandra Symonds, a New York psychiatrist who has studied dependency, and says it's a problem that affects most of the women she's ever met. Even those women who appear to be the most outwardly successful, she believes, tend to "subordinate themselves to others, become dependent on them, and quite unwittingly devote their major energies to the search for love, for help, for protection against that which is seen as difficult, or challenging, or hostile in the world." (http://www.colettedowling.com/work2.htm)

Bee, a successful novelist, told me how important it was for her to be with other achieving women:

> When my first book was published, it felt as if I'd broken through the surface of the water and into the light; However bad things might be in the future, I knew I'd never return to the dark place where I'd been for years, with endless rejections. Now I enjoy being with other women who've also been fortunate enough to achieve something in their lives. It's about realising potential – very often that is what success and failure are about, not about how good you are at something, but whether you get the chance to see it through, and have some recognition. And part of that is simply luck, and part of it is sheer bloody mindedness, refusing to accept defeat.

The effects of gender discrimination are not confined to women. Success, in terms of work achievement, has been traditionally demanded more of men than of women, and that is not always easy to accept. As William Leith put it in *The Times* magazine in November 2010, "If women have been judged as sex objects, men have been judged too – as success objects."

Competition

Although levels vary among individuals, competitiveness is rife in the human animal, especially when young. I'm embarrassed to acknowledge my own competitive streak. Even now, in competitions that I watch – whether quizzes, a cricket match or a singing contest – I need to be partisan to maintain a keen interest. Even if I'm not personally involved, I need to decide to support a particular individual or team. I want someone to *win*! Although the reason I am watching is generally because of an interest in the specific activity, I have to say that just watching the game is not enough. The kick of adrenalin caused by competitiveness, even at one remove, is addictive.

Competition dominates every field of life, from academic achievement to playground games, from the board room to the bedroom. More, better, bigger, faster: notches on the gun. Success is not always just about proving ourselves but defeating others. An athletics coach spoke of the young people with whom she works: "Yes, pb [personal best] matters but", with emphasis, "they want to win. Oh yes, they want to win!" The message from an advertisement shown on TV during the Atlanta Olympics was: "You don't win silver. You lose gold." One of the most often quoted aphorisms in American football is "Winning is not the most important thing. It's the only thing."

Sometimes success means defeating others, but even when there is no innate competitive dimension, as in a fine theatrical or musical performance or piece of writing, there seems to be a need to introduce one by giving awards and prizes: BAFTAS, Grammys, the Man Booker Book of the Year. Such competitions, although bringing welcome income to artists, can inhibit our appreciation of a work of art for what it is – a singular expression of the creative spirit. We apply the terms "matchless" and "incomparable" only to a few works of art, but to make a comparison suggests relation to some uniform standard, and denies the rich diversity of the gifts manifested and the uniqueness of each.

Even if the competition is not direct, there is only so much room at the top of the tree – whether the product is an electronic device or a piano recital. Actors compete for parts; charities vie for available funding; manufacturers for market share; politicians for parliamentary seats. We're all at it. Wherever there is a contest, the same event – a race, a match, a competition – will be a success for some, a failure for others. When someone wins, someone else has to lose.

Although the quality of what we do will often be judged against our own or others' expectations, it is important to distinguish between beating others and producing quality work. Beating others is, as Alfie Kohn argues in his book, *No Contest*, something quite different. According to Kohn, competition is not innate but culturally induced. He feels that competitive behaviour is "inherently destructive... counter-productive, and causes anxiety, selfishness, self-doubt, and poor communication".

I recently watched a little scene of three small children in a park. Two were of about the same age – say 8 years old – the third was several years younger. The three of them set off in a race, and the two older children were soon streets ahead. Ignoring the youngest child, one delightedly shouted out: "I won. Tom lost." The little one flung himself into his mother's arms, howling with frustration. But after a while he pulled himself together, turned round and ran the race on his own. When he had reached the end, he turned with a triumphant grin. "Never mind the others," his expression said. "I won."

Rewards

The rewards of success include recognition, congratulation and, for some, fame. More tangible rewards include prizes, certificates, promotion, honours and, of course, money. *Punished by Rewards*, also by Kohn, puts forward reasons to distrust the whole concept. Not only are rewards an example of short-termism, he says, but they are both morally dubious and ineffective in the long term. Whether applied to incentive payments, bribes, gold stars or even praise, he sees them as tools of control and, in the end, de-motivating.

It is certainly true that being paid for something changes the experience. In two instances, work I did first as a volunteer was turned into a paying job. There is no question about the fact that I felt more comfortable about being a volunteer. Once money entered into the equation, I became a little distracted from the job in hand: aware of what the expectations were and the number of hours I was supposed to work. As a volunteer, my motivation was clear: I was doing it for no other reason than because I wanted to. Perhaps, as Kohn says, "pay-for-performance is an inherently flawed concept" (2000:183). He suggests that we "*decouple the compensation from the task*" (original italics). In his view, the problem is not money itself but the fact that we pay it too much attention.

I still work as a volunteer facilitator for a conflict resolution programme. It is important for the ethos of the workshops that no one is paid. We are all – participants and facilitators – there because we want to be there, and for no other reason. Participants particularly value the fact that facilitators are prepared to give their time. If we were paid, their responses to the workshops would be more complex.

But the effect of even the most blatant of rewards can be more subtle. The most direct form of reward for sales people is commission. You get a cut from the proceeds of what you sell. A former entertainer I spoke to liked to have something of the same direct relationship with his public. Towards the end of a forty-year career, he enjoyed doing his own bookings – it felt like a success. He much preferred having no wages, but having his income dictated by the number of people who turned up. It was, he said, an honest way of earning a living.

A former senior civil servant said that the pay scale bore no relation to the amount or quality of work people actually did. The rewards were promotion, and the appreciation of others. She wasn't particularly interested in the praise of politicians or those senior to her, but she was gratified when her staff appreciated her, and most of all when she saw them blossom.

For some kinds of success – giving up smoking or losing weight, for instance – the reward will be an enhanced sense of wellbeing. For poet, Frances, "the reward is in the making. God has given me the tools, and I'm never happier than when practising my craft."

When Geoffrey, a statistician, left public service, he found he was lower down the hierarchy than fifteen years before, because they had introduced another level of management above him. He said, "I was quite taken aback to discover how important the matter of success, of position in the hierarchy, was." Yes, he did mind. "It increased my disgruntlement. There were more people telling me what to do; it was harder to get to the people making decisions. The message in the hidden script that got through to me was that rising up your profession or organisation was success."

"And did you accept it?"

"Yes, if I'd stayed an academic statistician, I would have felt that it was the senior statistician who knew his stuff, was respected."

Success is short-lived

We have this idea of success as an end-point, an ultimate arrival. But in fact history shows us that the heady heights of success – whether passing an exam, achieving a goal, or the reign of a celebrity – usually don't last. Comparative and longitudinal studies have shown that even organisations which have been at the top of the tree can sink into oblivion, either because they are not as good as they were, because others are better, or because times have changed. Some occupations, products, and the companies making and selling them, are limited by their time and place. Think of blacksmiths, typewriters or audio cassettes.

Although some individuals manage to maintain success in their chosen field, no one can rest on their laurels. We are only as good as our last performance. What's in, what's out, are notoriously transitory; our favours change with promiscuous ease.

In business, an emphasis on short-lived success can be destructive. In a discussion on the BBC World Service, the managing director of one of the world's largest management consultancy firms discussed with others the problem of short-termism. He said that CEOs of public companies are under pressure from investors to give quarterly returns; those playing the stock market want to move quickly, have an eye to the flicker of a trend, a quick success, a quick buck. This, he argues, is not only time-consuming and stressful for staff, but leads to short-termism that is damaging to the long-term future of businesses and can result in a distortion of the real picture. In Asia, we heard, it is more usual in government and in business to think in terms of decades – even looking to see where a business will be in sixty years' time. After all, we were told, businesses can take five to seven years to build.

As we will see in Chapter 12, the same could be said to be true in every avenue of life. Success is not about a quick fix, but a more deeply rooted and lasting sustainability. In health, in education, in the charitable sector, in our personal lives: however seductive we might find a quick injection of excitement, what we really want is something lasting and meaningful, something beyond the peaks and troughs of temporary losses and gains.

Being a success

In researching this book, it has been surprisingly hard to find people who regard themselves as successful. Even if all external factors suggest success in current worldly terms – maybe they are high up in a work hierarchy, earn a six-figure salary, command a high standard of living – most people are all too aware of their own fallibility. Andy has a home in London and three in the West Country, two of which are let. He lives in a house, does it up, then moves on; the use of a building changes from home to being part of a business. Andy has had several businesses since being made redundant about thirty years ago, beginning with the acquisition of a small firm that had failed. He has worked in the US and in the City; he has run factories and worked in import, export, and retail consulting. He developed one of his businesses from his back room to a brand name; the number of employees grew from 2 people to 120. It now employs about 90 plus 40 or 50 indirectly. Andy is now a multi-millionaire but does not consider himself as successful. As he looked at his life, he made an interesting contribution to the debate:

> Forgot to say that because of illness and failing to get my plan of a number of businesses under one holding company I'm now wrapping them up bit by bit – my wealth has dropped by approx £4m. It's interesting – at one level I've failed, at another I'm trying and – bit by bit – succeeding in changing my life to give it a different focus and meaning (though still business orientated out of necessity for a while at least). I still of course own a business with a turnover of about £9m (it was £13m) and 100 and 85 or so employees but ... have I failed? My wealth creation aim has and jobs have inevitably been lost and I pay less tax (I see tax a contribution to the community pot).

It's common even for people who have achieved a great deal in their careers to feel a fraud, to feel that some day they are going to be found out. A poet actually used the word "fraud" to express how she felt. Every time she sits down to write, she feels: "I've never written a poem, or I'll never write another, and what am I doing here?" Many people, it seems, suffer from a minor form of the psychological phenomenon known as "the impostor syndrome", in which people are unable to internalise their accomplishments. Regardless of what level of success they may have achieved in their chosen field of work or study or what external proof they may have of their competence, those with the syndrome remain convinced internally they do not deserve the success they have achieved and are actually frauds. Proof of success is dismissed as luck, timing, or as a result of deceiving others into thinking they were more intelligent and competent than they believe themselves to be. (Wikipedia)

Maybe success is something for others. When I asked my neighbour Valerie what the word success brought to mind, she said,

Sitting in the bus and thinking about it, I realised that I see all my friends as very successful people, my brother and sister too, incredibly successful. I don't see the things that they haven't achieved or had wanted to. But it's different with myself.

People are not good at judging their own work. Speaking from my experience of being an editor, agent and, now, author, I know that it usually takes an outsider to see the wood for the trees. The history books are full of people who did not understand where their success lay. Richmal Crompton, for instance, is famed for her Just William books for children, but she considered that it was her books for adults, now largely forgotten, that mattered.

Fear of success

In some countries, it is dangerous to do well, and any fear of success is well founded. Anyone standing out in any way in Zimbabwe, for instance, is an object of suspicion to the authorities, who might well come to investigate the reasons for your success. Sometimes the problem is more local. In South Africa, one of our microcredit clients was doing well at her fabric softener business. By the third week of our meetings, she had not only produced a saleable product, but had obtained some orders. As time went on, the local B&B establishments agreed to buy her product when their stocks ran out, and the hospital was next on the agenda. To begin with, customers brought their own containers for her to fill; she then began to buy second-hand bottles. The next step would be to buy new containers, then to design her own label, so that she could offer her product to local, then national, shops.

However, at one meeting she announced that she was not prepared to continue. She lived alone, and too much success, she said, would make her a target for crime. When we confronted the local municipality with the need to do something about the level of crime in the area, they denied it. The breakthrough came from the woman's microcredit group who suggested that the business should nominally employ them. In that way the danger of attack would be spread.

But, in general, fear of success has little to do with external conditions. As Marianne Williamson has written in a piece made famous by Nelson Mandela:

> Our deepest fear is not that we are inadequate, our deepest fear is that we are powerful beyond measure. It is our light, not our darkness that most frightens us. We ask ourselves, "Who am I to be brilliant, gorgeous, talented and fabulous?"

As well as fear of failure, it can be fear of success that stops us doing something altogether or prevents us doing it in such a way that it reaches its full potential, or indeed allows us to fulfil our own. My own focus has been to get things off the ground, to work with beginners, to start small. This was true of my literary agency, where I specialised in first-time novelists, and later with microcredit, starting with little money, a few women, a small community, and allowing ripples to spread. Does this show a lack of ambition or a fear of success? Or of failure?

Barbara's career has taken the opposite path. She describes her life as a deliberate high-risk strategy, always going to the limits. She has now, she says, reached them and is glad. "I wouldn't have wanted to die without testing my limits." However, "the problem with always going for something that would help one million people, not ten people, means the chance of succeeding gets smaller and smaller."

In the UK we have a strange attitude to personal success. If we hide our failures, we certainly do not parade our successes. Diffidence, false humility, is the acceptable attitude, sometimes with a jocular undercutting of our achievements. A priest told me that "to claim success embarrasses me". Hiding one's light under a bushel is perhaps a peculiarly British tendency: it's not done to show off. For some reason, an exception is made for sports interviews, in which players routinely tell us how well they have played, what good form they are on. They are expected to analyse their successes and strut their stuff. Why is boasting acceptable in this arena and not in others? Certainly North Americans have fewer inhibitions about doing things on a large scale, and of being seen to succeed. One woman told me that the reason she emigrated to Canada at the age of twenty-one was that she felt that there she would be able to be her biggest self, that she would not have to pretend or shrink herself to fit into a socially acceptable mould.

The cost of success

Success can demand sacrifices. Parents will sacrifice much to ensure their children get a good education; in some cases, they give up years of their lives to enable the success of a child in ballet, acting or sport, accompanying their offspring to auditions, coaching or lessons – sometimes dedicating their own lives to tuition. In the protagonist, success demands attention, focus, often an increasingly narrow specialisation that shuts out the development of other talents. For every door to open wide to success, others will have to close, and sometimes that is a hard price to pay.

A businessman told me that failure is easier, clean. "Success causes problems: it becomes real. You have to start thinking about how do I raise the finance, manage growth and so on." In his 2010 Free Thinking lecture for BBC radio 4, Frank Cottrell Boyce gave a similar opinion. If success comes early, you have to deal with it. People, he says, can be undone by success – it can trap you, define you, especially if it's not the success you wanted it to be. For success can take you by surprise. Something that started as a modest affair may grow beyond our wildest imaginings, or in unexpected directions. And the results may not always be welcome.

Continuing success

Andrew is a much sought-after hairdresser. For some years he had his own salon, but, finding the responsibility and administration more than he wanted, he gave it up. Cutting hair is what he loves, not management. Andrew does not consider this decision to have made him a failure. He trained a number of people and gave them employment; giving up the salon was his choice. It is easier, he feels, to make do with moderate success. As he saw clearly, the problem with success is to remain successful. The choice was to keep going at that level, or perpetually to be in a process of growth. Indeed, keeping a business at a static level is almost impossible. It has to grow or it stagnates. As any owner of a business will tell you, managing size and growth is one of the hardest parts of the job. As Irving Berlin said, "The toughest thing about success is that you've got to keep on being a success."

In some cases, the need to keep going is provoked not by an inner need, but by the huge unmet need in the world at large.

One woman who has spent over twenty years as a social activist said, "What if you just can't carry on any more? There's so much more to do. Is that failure? We can't cure everything. We do our best."

* * *

In an objective sense, success and failure might seem to be pretty clear cut: you either pass or fail an exam; you either win or lose a race. But did you get 60% or 80%? By how much did you win the race? Was it a personal best? Even in the starkest examples, there are shades of grey. It is possible to pluck failure from the jaws of success. And the reverse. Even if I fail an exam, or lose a race, if I do better than before, it is some kind of success.

Success and failure do not exist in their own right, but only in relation to each other and to some kind of measure or expectation by self or others. Where do we set our benchmark? What is the pass level? Is the expectation set by others or by a sense of our own capability or potential? Let us look now at how we measure success.

3

Measuring success

My first approach to the Anglican priest, Father James, came, it seems, at an interesting time. His inner-city parish had just had a visit from a theological college. Unexpectedly, the questions they set the students included:

1. How do you measure success?
2. What do you consider a successful priest?

One might wonder why it is important to measure what priests do, and it is certainly true that much of what they do cannot be measured, but in the context of the expense of a big church being open all day, and the capacity of the building to produce income for them, such seemingly secular questions as how many candles have been lit, how many people are likely to have come in, have some relevance. When pushed, Father James admitted that his own measures might include the fact that congregations have grown, churches have grown stronger, there is a broader base of leadership, more people feel welcome, and there is more diversity in the congregation.

Tick boxes and targets

In any sector of the working world it is hard to get away from assessment. Businesses are evaluated according to market share, return on assets, and percentage of return on turnover. Schools and hospitals are assessed according to their place in league tables. And the work of individuals is continually under examination. It used to be the case that after stressful milestones such as school and college exams and job interviews, many people could simply get on with their work, do what they did. Now, and especially at a time of less job security, everyone is tested, assessed and supervised. There are Ofsted inspections even for dance evening classes.

The voluntary sector is not immune from continuous assessment. Indeed, an entrepreneur told me that at international conventions you could always tell people from the charitable sector: they were the ones who were most formally dressed, and preoccupied with documentation and money. He worried that their energy was going into tick-boxes and paperwork rather than into more subjective outcomes.

Most organisations, public, private and charitable, mark progress by monitoring, evaluation and, most of all, by setting and seeking to reach targets, increasingly those prescribed by funders. Outputs can be hard to measure, even if a funder understands that tick boxes are a crude measure, and has some understanding of the softer outcomes that are a truer assessment of progress in developmental programmes.

It was refreshing to meet Abby, who for the past eight years has worked as an independent consultant and project manager, a "trouble-shooter" called in to put in processes, to advise on or implement alternative strategies. By the very nature of her job, all the companies she visits are in trouble but, somewhat surprisingly, her attitude and solutions are very human-based. Yes, she looks at resource allocation, recruitment practice and risk assessment, but she also talks to managers and to other staff: she finds out what it's like to work there, what the "vibe" is. Some managers need telling that it's the people in an organisation who make it what it is. Her solutions usually involve finding out about people's skills and suggesting roles that would most suit them. Success in a recession may simply consist in covering your costs and getting through it. But her definition of a successful company is not restricted to financial considerations, but is to do with making the workplace a better place, so that people want to stay. It's about getting the name of the company out there as one for which people want to work – so much is done by word of mouth, after all. Reports, yes, self-assessment, yes, but form-filling, Abby says, should always be backed up by a one-to-one conversation.

Even a statistician who used to work in the Audit Commission where evaluation was a central part of the work, commented on the limitation of targets. "I wanted to understand what was going on, why, for instance, three radiographers didn't get on with the other three." He needed to understand the process, and reacted against a culture that looked for 500 targets for each local authority, and where there was an ethos of "what can be measured gets done".

Valerie is a young hospital doctor who plays hockey in her spare time. She says that everything she does is very objective: "You win or you lose; you succeed or fail. I can see the outcome of everything I do." In medicine, she says, success is measured by progression. "Medics are very competitive. Academia is a tick-box exercise – getting GCSEs, "A" levels and degree under your belt." But, personally, she says she is not competitive in her career, happy for everyone to do well, and she recognises that "your personality and getting on with people will get you jobs. Common sense and being a balanced person are more important."

Penny, who worked in a human resources department in the corporate sector before working for a charity, says that she learnt a good deal from the experience. One particular method of appraisal that particularly interested her was 360° feedback, in which the manager, peers and subordinates of a member of staff rate their performance and attitudes. It can, as she says, indicate improvements in performance (and therefore success) in terms of hard measures such as number of sales made, reports written. But the measures more usually include aspects of personality, or at least personal interaction, and with these it can be that the person realises that how they see themselves and how they are seen by others can be very different, which could lead to wanting to change/improve your interactions with others in order to bring them closer into alignment. Or maybe realising that in order to be a more effective manager or team player you need to adjust aspects of your interactions/personality. And so, on re-assessment, these may change, which would indicate success in adapting your style.

Eight years after her Reith lectures on trust, moral philosopher Professor Onora O'Neill revisited the subject in 2011 for an Analysis programme on BBC radio. She felt that tick-boxes did not provide a system of assessment that was efficient or encouraged trust. Although they might be useful to denote the performance of limited actions – a toilet that has been cleaned, for instance (although even then a tick will say nothing about the quality of the cleaning) – their use in appraising education, the health service or the police is inadequate. She felt that in education, for instance, a parent would not gain sufficient information or be able to trust the outcome from a list of exam results, or a school's place in the league tables. In practice, she feels that most people, using their own common sense, investigate the suitability of a school both by examining its exam results and by talking to teachers or other parents. Success, in other words, does not depend on a list of numbers. The human factor is essential. Professor O'Neill said that she felt that the pre-eminence of league tables had driven schools to ignore their responsibility to a wide range of children: "The assessment tail is wagging the education dog."

We have become accustomed to everything being measurable, dominated by hierarchy, winners and losers. The use of the word "customer" applied to train travel, education and health, is a symptom of how the market and target culture has been extended into inappropriate areas, turning human beings into fodder for someone else's statistics.

Work in the voluntary sector has changed. According to a woman who has worked for some years in the homelessness sector, it used to be possible to apply for funding without having to provide evidence of success. In the present focus on proof, funders – and especially government funders – now require organisations working with homeless people to demonstrate progress. They need to prove that housing has been found, rehab., where necessary, sorted; measurable outcomes have been achieved, people "moved on". Although everyone wants progress of this kind, it isn't always possible. Demands for it can be a denial of the complexities of working with this client group. The effect on the charity is an increased work-load in the production of evidence, anxiety about the continuity of programmes and, worryingly, a frequent perceived need to tailor what the charity does to suit funding requirements. Most importantly, target-driven priorities lead to a tendency, conscious or not, to pick the clients most likely to be helped successfully (for instance, housed) instead of those in greatest need.

Organisations working with the Prison Service suffer from the same problem when they are required to demonstrate how their work has reduced re-offending. It is hard to see that as a measurable outcome, when a programme is only one of many experienced by prisoners, and the tracing of prisoners after release is notoriously difficult.

Much charitable and social work is simply not suitable for external assessment. In the mental health field, drop-in centres have become unfashionable, as they do not demonstrate progress: it's "only" ill people talking to ill people. But achievement can be at a very basic, and profound, level. Maybe, a mental health chaplain said, going to a centre is all that some people can cope with; it is something. Just to keep going is something to be proud of. Sometimes success is just staying alive. She commented on the adverse effect of funding requirements: the success rate for addiction programmes, it seems, is low, setting up a vicious circle of failure. There is lack of success, therefore there is little funding, therefore there is lack of success. Alcoholics Anonymous, however, is free, and seems to work.

A therapist stressed the importance of thinking about how we measure success. She too regretted the intrusion of business-based criteria. What was fundamental to her work, she said, was simply to "do no harm", and to recognise that we can't heal everything.

Tick box evaluation provides an external, partial and de-personalising viewpoint. If a business or a charity reaches its target for the year, or for a particular project, it can be seen as a success. But one can tick all the boxes and still not be a success in broader, deeper terms, if the human aspect or the long-term impact has been ignored. When the focus is entirely on material outcomes, in whatever field, the human collateral damage is ignored. Despite casualties, battles are "won"; asset-stripping and creating unemployment are considered to "save" businesses.

In medicine, too, judging an outcome as success may be a limited viewpoint. "Success" in cancer treatment can mean a brutal process in which radiation and drugs attack parts of the body. A successful result in treating a specific illness may come at the cost of a decline in general health. Too often taking one drug results in the need to take others to deal with the side-effects of the first. Specialisation is at the core of orthodox Western medicine. A specialist will be concerned with the health of a part of the human body: a limb, an eye or the colon, and take little interest in the rest of the body except as it impinges on the part under consideration. Even a general practitioner is likely to compartmentalise her attention, not necessarily making the connection between symptoms in different parts of the body or an emotional state. One respondent told a story of a geriatric consultant who had said to him, without irony, "I have too many unprofitable patients", and followed the story by quoting: "The operation was successful, but the patient died".

On the other hand, holistic medicine by its very nature seeks to treat the emotional and physical entity of a patient. The process is a therapeutic one. When I asked my homeopath about a friend of mine who had been told that her cancer was terminal, she said that she couldn't change the end result, but could strengthen my friend in what she would have to undergo: to improve the quality of what remained of her life. What she offered was a different kind of success.

Education

Many people working within systems under increasingly stringent controls are finding it hard to continue. Teachers are leaving the profession not just because of the burden of paperwork, but because they do not believe in the superficial criteria for assessment or in targets that have little to do with the innate development of the child. A lot of children, said one teacher, arrive at school already with the idea that this is something they're not good at, a view that often becomes a self-fulfilling prophecy.

Frankie remembers the appalling division created by the 11+ exam. It never occurred to her family that any of them would fail, but her brother did. She remembered the morning assembly at which the headmaster announced: "These children have failed", and her brother's name was among those read out. He went, she said, to "some crummy school" until her parents found the money to send him to a little private school where he acquired "a veneer of respectability".

Even though the 11+ has largely disappeared, the current state system tests children as young as 6. At the end of Year 1, children are tested on reading; the following year, for Key Stage 1 SATS, children are assessed by tests and teacher assessment. Key Stage

2 SATS takes place at 11, with an exam and some teacher assessment. As children get older, in an increasingly competitive arena, the importance of exam grades is emphasised, grades that later in life usually have no meaning. As senior lecturer Susan Greenberg writes, "a grade can only offer a snapshot in time, rather than a definitive statement about a work's potential" (in Hillson, 59). The stress caused by frequent testing at young ages cannot be overstated.

Paul, a life-long teacher, explained in a letter to the *Independent* his reasons for leaving the profession. "Schools have become exam factories." He described a meeting he had with an assistant headteacher about improving exam grades. When Paul pointed out that the exam was so easy a primary school student could pass it, the assistant head said, "It isn't about what they learn; it's about what grade they get." That comment, Paul said, was the final straw (26 March 2011).

The private system, of course, has advantages. Richard's experience of nearly forty years' teaching the International Baccalaureate (IB) in an international school is instructive. The only external exam is the IB itself; otherwise, reports are made to the parents three times a year, based on the pupils' work and their attitude to work. The school is not subject to the National Curriculum; outlines and assessment of course material come from outside but the content is determined by the school – determined collectively by the staff, with cross-links between subjects. Ofsted has the responsibility for assessing duty of care, health and safety; accreditation is conducted by the Council of International Schools, an offshoot of the European Council of International Schools, and the IB itself. The IB's aim is to produce a rounded child, which they define by what is called "the learner profile":

IB learners strive to be:
- inquirers

- knowledgeable
- thinkers
- communicators
- principled
- open-minded
- caring
- risk-takers
- balanced
- reflective.

Richard is wary of these definitions, considering them as purely Western norms. In a school of some fifty nationalities, not all of these concepts would be universally accepted. For instance, he says, "risk-taking" is not a quality that would appeal to Asian families, and you only have to compare this list with Amy Chua's views in Chapter 2 to see how wide the differences can be. Richard is keen on the idea of self-inspection in the school, keen that they establish for themselves something more generally acceptable. "What is it that we intend? What can we agree on as an institution?" You need to start with the purpose, he says. Aim is the way; the rules the conclusion. He is concerned that "we always start with the rules instead of the purpose".

Some people are good at exams; I am not; I am nervous and have always disliked them. At the 11+, I turned over two pages at once in one of the papers and although I passed, did not do well enough to go to my chosen school. Although I learned the piano for five years or so, I always refused to take exams: I wanted piano-playing to remain a pleasure. After graduating, I shrank from applying for an attractive job in Brussels, because it would have meant taking an exam and, although I did the course for the fellowship of the Institute of Linguists, I funked the exam. I simply could not have borne to sit another. It was more than dislike: it was a nervous inability to put myself through another such ordeal.

Self-employment, although stressful, can be an oasis from outside assessment. I ran my own business for fourteen years. It was a small but successful literary agency – we were well thought of, made money and enjoyed ourselves. We were answerable to our clients (they would leave if they weren't satisfied), and worked effectively and professionally, but the work was immensely personal: everything depended on the relationship between agent and author, and agent and publisher. I had to make sure we covered our overheads, and I did set a target each year, but it was pretty elastic. Representing authors, human beings – and creative ones at that – cannot be an exact science. Sometimes a book would sell in one financial year, sometimes the following month. Or the deal would be done in one year and the advance come in in the next. And no one can tell how well a book will sell. Generally things balanced each other out. Staff of the agency were self-employed. Each had her area of work, and got on with it. Occasionally I looked over my shoulder at bigger agencies making huge sums for their authors, but not often. We were just different, with our own specific skills and contributions. Our authors had long-term careers with good reputations, and many made a comfortable living from their writing. Horses for courses.

* * *

So far, we have explored the concept of success from the outside, as if it had an objective identity. And, indeed, our society behaves as if it does. Education, public life, business and much of the voluntary sector make absolute judgements on a daily basis. But as we consider the subject, it becomes clear that in some cases attaching the labels of success and failure is a subjective matter. Either label might be applied to the same circumstance, depending on the point of view, or indeed the same individual may view an event differently at the time and years afterwards.

Softer outcomes

In recognition of the importance of the process, some trusts and foundations are unwilling to see simplistic "success" and "failure" as appropriate concepts. This is not only because these ideas can be so exposing and so wounding to people who have done their best, but because nuance matters. The Quaker Joseph Rowntree Charitable Trust (JRCT) occasionally hires external evaluators to look at some of the work they fund, but in general, says one trustee, the work they fund does not have "nicely countable outputs". They make a "qualitative judgement", helped by the fact that they make a point of getting to know the people and the organisation. If they are not sure, they might fund some research to begin with, and then fund further stages. Some projects take longer than expected, but it was hard, she said, to think of something that could be counted as a failure.

To celebrate their centenary in 2004, JRCT appointed seven Rowntree Visionaries for a Just and Peaceful World (two working as a job-share). The evaluation process (or lack of it) is instructive.

Surprisingly, the scheme had no plans for a formal evaluation of outcomes. Trustees were keen to avoid the well-worn funding path of "I don't want to burden you", followed by a bewildering array of differing reporting forms and structures. They also wanted to avoid the paraphernalia of self-serving evaluations not really done for objective learning.

Instead a simple system was developed of bi-annual reports from the project co-ordinator, who kept in regular friendly touch with the Visionaries, and an annual review with each individual – for which the Visionary provided in advance a written report in an agreed format. (Rosemary Hartill, forthcoming report)

Because the Visionaries were working on different size canvases, trustees felt it might be misleading to compare achievements too closely. Some work in a domestic, others in an international, arena. Achievements may happen quickly, or after years.

Asked to comment on the reporting process, one of the Visionaries felt that the process had "lacked a certain rigour and accountability" and others commented that they would have welcomed more challenge, and having an external mentor would have helped. Rosemary Hartill commented that "the effectiveness of the kind of process JRCT adopted does rather depend on the rigour and objectivity of the project co-ordinator's reports. That can sometimes be difficult to maintain when the co-ordinator's job is also to support and care for the individuals."

In her book, *Just Change*, Diana Leat explores other reasons why assessing success in the area of development is not simple:

- Intervening near the end of a process when an issue is already firmly on the public agenda is quite different from getting an issue onto the agenda in the first place.
- Some causes evoke unpopularity, the sense of being neglected or attracting hostility. But in some respects it is easier to work with contentious issues, because some people will feel passionately. Working in the corridors of indifference can be disheartening.
- Success also depends on who or what needs to change. Some industries are notoriously resistant to change, others less so.
- Success is relative in terms of its scale. How can one compare work which has high impact on grantees, but lesser impact way beyond immediate grantees?
- What has been the price of success? Has there been collateral damage?

Among the underlying values quoted by JRCT are:

- Taking risks – recognising that risking failure is necessary to achieve outstanding success. [See Chapter 5 of this book for a fuller discussion.]

- Recognising that how things are done is often as important as what is done.
- Trying to be humble – recognising that it may be possible to be mistaken.
- Achieving longer term systemic change with impact beyond immediate grantees, and inspire practice. These include the importance of:

    flexibility, opportunism and luck (and implications for core funding)

    passion

    creating an evidence base/credible knowledge

    telling human stories

    reframing and relating to other agendas

    working on different fronts

    dissemination and tailoring communications to audience needs

    providing "easy"/"smart" answers

    focusing on the positive/constructive

    presenting clear and simple messages

    focus on the message not the messenger

    going to where the power to effect change lies

    building legitimacy, anticipating obstacles and recruiting champions

    focus on the outcome

    persistence

    key individuals.

    http://www.jrct-visionaries.org.uk

Directly attributable outcomes, they say, are often difficult to measure and pin down to specific timetables. It is easy to give in to short-termism.

Foundations have an understandable desire to see "results"...Change generally requires time spans that are longer than many foundations are prepared to commit to. Again this may create a vicious circle in which foundations are reluctant to embark on, say, 10 year commitments; or, when they do engage with change projects, fund for too short a time and are then disappointed with the lack of clear results.

Foundations need...inspiring examples of success (and lessons from "failure"). They need to be able to remind each other that achieving change may be difficult, uncertain and slow but if it achieves wider, more sustainable impact then it may be no more uncertain, slow and costly than year after year of grantmaking to achieve short-term assistance which is constantly in need of renewal. (Leat, 20)

There is also an issue about what counts as success. Success was defined broadly to include more interest and awareness about an issue, policy change and effective implementation. Clearly, measuring/seeing policy change is easier than measuring interest and awareness, and effective implementation. We were also conscious that it would be all too easy to focus on policy change and to neglect the less tangible, less dramatic, equally important, longer term matter of effective implementation of policy. (*ibid*., 22)

For the last ten years, I have been involved in setting up microcredit programmes in various parts of the world. Microcredit is a particular model of lending small amounts of money to individuals (mainly women) living in poverty to start enterprises. No collateral is asked for, just the commitment of joining a group, usually of five, each with her own business idea, and meeting on a regular basis. The group provides support and each woman guarantees the loans of the others in her group. The main focus is not on the idea or the business plan but on the human being. It is after all the person who will have to make it happen.

In microcredit programmes, measuring subtle outcomes is essential. One tool that we created was an action sheet, a more subtle form of tick-box, which clients filled in at the beginning of the programme, then after six months, and a year. It consists of a list of actions to tick, which in our programme in the East End of London, a programme that included 22 nationalities in its first year, included using a telephone directory or an A-Z map of London. In other countries it begins with "Used a phone", "Learnt to read". Later questions include "Told my family about my business idea" and "Joined a group" right through to "Got my own business bank account", "Created a website for my business".

Not only does it enable project workers and clients themselves to see their progress as more actions are ticked, but it educates funders about the subtle successes of growing self-esteem and confidence.

In fact, achieving any of these milestones could be considered a success. For microcredit is not, at root, about money. Repayment rates are of course crucial and the number of loans matters, but even those who don't take a loan, who start a business without one, or leave the programme before starting a business, have been helped. We certainly hear stories of people whose increased confidence has enabled them to get a job, or to go into further education. The training is never wasted, nor is the bonding between members of the groups: friendship, reduction of isolation, possible sharing of resources, childcare, and, most of all, self-belief – these too must be regarded as success.

Sharing

Even if star-struck audiences celebrate the prowess of individual players, the point of team sports is that they operate on a collaborative basis. The success of the winning 2011 English cricket team, for instance, was largely due to the discipline and collective spirit of the team, rather than the performance of any individual player. Over a period, in any successful team, many players will shine, morale will be high, and it is the collective reputation that benefits.

A more collaborative culture that runs counter to celebrity notions of success can be seen in many areas of life: not only in many voluntary sector organisations, but in public service too. In her examination of how success is assessed, Diana Leat includes: "Accept that success has many parents – don't expect to be a lone heroine...Work collaboratively" (10). In his 2010 Free Thinking festival lecture on "The joys of failure", Frank Cottrell Boyce also plays down the need for public recognition: "There is no end to what we can do if we are not bothered about who takes the credit." Several of the people I spoke to took collective credit for granted. Geoffrey sees himself as a team player. He objects to the kinds of questions on job applications such as "what is your greatest success; what have you achieved?" "The implication is that it's me personally. It was me with others. Taking credit collectively." The same is true, he feels, in his position as a trustee. Any "success" that they feel has been achieved in an area that is "more stable, more thought through" is collective. And when I reminded William that he helped a lot of people by his work in the local neighbourhood association, he said, "Yes, I suppose we do". We. He didn't see it as a personal achievement.

Scientific research, of course, is a team effort, both at any one time, and across the generations. "You stand", as they say, "on the shoulders of giants." As Alfie Kohn says in his book about rewards, "excellence" in many areas "is often the product of cooperation, and even individual achievement typically is built on the work of other people's earlier efforts. So who 'deserves' the reward when lots of people had a hand in the performance?" (2000: 21)

A woman who runs an international charity takes it one step further. "I've thought a lot about credit: if you've done something well, you should try to give it away. It never goes away. You don't mean to keep the credit, but somehow it both sticks and multiplies." Having worked as an advisor to managers on strategic development before running her own charity, she has found it true in both fields. "I used it in management, with brilliant results. People you give it to perform better. It's also a way to get a voluntary organisation to work."

Although the current emphasis on intellectual property means that there is often a desire to claim ideas and reject the contributions of others to the final result, the truth is that inventions, innovation, creative ideas are often part of a continuum, a process. Great art, music or literature, for instance, is part of a tradition, building on what has gone before. As Boyce says, "brilliant ideas come incrementally". Often the person celebrated for a discovery may only have been a link in the chain. As we will explore more deeply in Chapter 6, your failure may be someone else's success.

4

Failure

Failure occurs at the point where we stop succeeding. (David Hillson)

There is no success without failure. Like all pairs of opposites – good/evil, light/dark – each serves to define the other, to set it into sharper focus.

Going back to the Oxford English Dictionary, we find that the current objective definitions of failure are "non-performance, default" or "want of success". The second meaning is the one most in use, but it is worth looking at the first. Never actually doing something is to fail to do it, but actually it does not risk failure, or indeed success, in its execution. It is easier to live in dreams: you can't fail if you never begin. In a self-destructive kind of way, "circumstances beyond your control" can always stop you doing something.

Elizabeth Evitts Dickinson writes on the Observatory website:

> The biggest failures may be the hidden ones, the ones born of atrophy. In a goal-oriented culture such as ours, production and output often outweigh genuine creative process. A fear of failure may be based, in part, in a fear of not producing.

Someone in the charitable sector told me that it's sometimes hard to put your finger on why something isn't happening, why one fails to take the last step. Sometimes it's important to wait. Maybe there's a lack of clarity about what it is that you want to do. Not doing something may not be a failure but a sensible decision, a piece of discernment that the time is not ripe, the programme is not appropriate or, in personal terms, it simply isn't a priority, it doesn't matter that much. William, for instance, began a law conversion course, but decided not to continue. The pressure of disciplined memorising was something he did not feel equipped to do: he did not see it as a failure, but a realistic appraisal. Geoffrey began a PhD but gave it up when he needed to find a job. He did not feel strongly enough about continuing to commit long hours to work and study at the same time and, having learnt a good deal in the process, does not regard it as a failure. Susan, however, does have one regret about leaving the civil service in her mid-forties. Having been deputy head of several units, she feels that she could have moved to a senior position, broken through the glass ceiling, and provided a role model and a path finder for other women. Although she did not fail in execution, she feels that she failed to push to the limit.

In general, though, the word "failure" implies something attempted that did not work. A failed project is seen as something that didn't hit the mark, didn't yield positive outcomes, or just wasn't good. It didn't come up to expectation; it didn't reach the level of continuity and scale that was hoped for. Matt Soar writes in his blog:

> The idea of failure seems to be straightforward enough: mistakes, both large and small, are something to be avoided; the opposite of success; the currency of losers. They're expected of the young as a necessary part of learning, of course, but increasingly less tolerated with the maturity that supposedly grants us enough experience and accumulated wisdom to succeed in life more or less flawlessly.
> http://observatory.designobserver.com/entry.html?entry=6627

But we all know that failure is an everyday occurrence. Not everything works; we don't get everything right all the time.

All of us screw up, misunderstand ideas, misjudge situations, underestimate other people, overestimate ourselves – and all of this over and over again! (Schulz, 198)

Messing up is a part of life. On the whole we shrug, sigh, swear perhaps, and try again or try something else.

There is a tendency to see failure and success as absolutes and make judgements accordingly but, as with all opposites, there are gradations on a spectrum between the two extremes. In his book, *Adapt*, Harford distinguishes three types of error:

The most straightforward are *slips*, when through clumsiness or lack of attention you do something you simply don't mean to do...Then there are *violations*, which involve someone deliberately doing the wrong thing... Most insidious are *mistakes*. Mistakes are things you do on purpose, but with unintended consequences, because your mental model of the world is wrong (original italics, 208).

Nonetheless, making a mistake is seen as being something less absolute than failure. Human error is permissible. Is it a matter of scale? Mary Pickford made a good point when she said, "If you have made mistakes, even serious ones, there is always another chance for you. What we call failure is not the falling down but the staying down." Accepting defeat is failure. We have always been bidden, after all, to pick ourselves up and start all over again. Churchill, who surprisingly had his own share of (largely forgotten) failures, put it another way: "Success consists of going from failure to failure without loss of enthusiasm." Many of life's failures come from people who did not realise how close they were to success when they gave up.

How failure, or the threat of it, is viewed can differ considerably, depending on the viewpoint. Ashanti Development is a small NGO in Ghana with a number of different programmes. It is well thought of and achieves a great deal for the residents of several villages. Among its achievements are the building of a health clinic, specialising in eye work; the provision of free school meals for the under-fives; free health insurance; and building wells and latrines together with local people. A recent addition to the work is a microcredit programme, providing business training and small loans to enable the women of a number of villages to enter self-employment. When news came that some of the women in one village were refusing to repay their loans, the director was quite matter-of-fact, and contemplated closing the programme. Her managerial view had to take into account the effectiveness and financial viability of the organisation as a whole. For her, she said it wouldn't have been devastating – "it was only one arm, and we would have turned it into something else".

I happened to be the person running the microcredit programme, and for me and the women on the programme it would, I think, have been devastating. My colleague and I had spent months training the women and the local worker. Expectations among the hundreds of women on the programme were high. With no possibility of employment in the area, and hardly any other income, this was a lifeline, their only possibility of a better life. What accentuated the problem for me was that I was at the time writing about the power of microcredit, and the strengths of the magnificent model started by the Grameen Bank in Bangladesh some thirty years before, on which my own work is based. How, in the circumstances, could I give examples of good practice, if my own programme was failing?

In the event, when my colleague and I returned to Ghana, the matter was easily resolved: the situation was not as dramatic as we had been led to believe. Poor communication and the barrier of different languages make misunderstanding all too easy. But if the programme had closed, the effect on the women would have been profound. They would have felt let down yet again; yet another hope would have been destroyed. It was the strength of my response to this event that led me to ponder more deeply the meaning of failure – and resulted in the writing of this book.

If being wrong is about facts and convictions, failure is about action – or the lack of it. It will involve being wrong: about the need, the circumstances, the necessary preparation, our ability or that of those working with us, our risk assessment, the process, or our adaptability. We too readily believe in our rightness, and that nothing will change. We need to be open to possibilities beyond those we can see at the outset.

We talked in an earlier chapter of the impostor syndrome, in which even gifted and experienced people cannot believe in their own success; they feel frauds. Sometimes, this attitude is not a fallacy but a realistic assessment of the ephemeral nature of success. Mark said that there are many in the entertainment business who are waiting to be found out. Meeting a group in Sydney, he asked what they were doing. From being well- known figures in the entertainment business, they were now doing a round of entertaining rugby clubs, and said: "We got found out." He quoted: "Be nice to people on the way up, because you'll meet them coming down."

One man I spoke to, who has suffered all his life from inter-mittent bouts of depression, took thirteen years to get his degree. Leaving the course part-way through his final year, he returned to it several times, before finally achieving an impressive 2:1 in politics and sociology. In February 2010, the *Daily Mail* quoted a study that revealed that those who pass their driving test on their second attempt have fewer points on their licence, are less likely to suffer road rage or be stopped by police, and have had the fewest accidents in the last five years. However, the research found that those who took more than two attempts to pass have not done so well. "Drivers who need a dismal four, five or six efforts before making the grade have the worst record behind the wheel." It is hard to imagine the quality of the driving of sixty-nine-year-old Cha Sa-soon from Jeonju, South Korea, who passed her driving test after 960 attempts.

Why did it fail?

In some arenas of life, success has to be taken for granted. Lack of success in flying an aeroplane is unimaginable. And in many medical operations, too, failure means death. Those carrying out these kinds of work live with the pressure to perform *every time*. In other arenas, failure is a daily occurrence. Artists live with failure both in the process of creation and in how it is received. Having tried, tried and tried again until what is produced is as near as possible to the original vision or to one transformed in the making, they are then subject to the continual rejection of an indifferent public. As one poet told me: "I could paper my walls with rejections."

But for many of us, failure is an occasional hiccough in the generally smooth progression of our lives. So, why do we or something we do fail? What went wrong? Maybe our expectations were too high; maybe the project was never suitable in the context, at that particular time and place, or there was a design fault in the programme. Maybe the choice of staff was not appropriate or inadequate monitoring allowed things to slip. Most of these errors can be put right.

Individually, failure – of an exam, for instance – is more personal. Maybe we simply aren't up to it. That's hard to swallow, and generally we try to protect our ego by finding other possibilities. Maybe we did not work hard enough; maybe we prepared for the wrong bits; maybe the examiner didn't see our original genius. Special pleading is natural enough.

The fear of failure

"Fear of failure is a big thing for me." Penny is a strong, motivated young woman with a Master's degree in occupational psychology. She comes from a family with high expectations, and she has high expectations of herself. As she says, "there's always the fear of not living up to them. If I'm anxious about something, or don't know what to do, I put it off. It's paralysing." She doesn't like to reveal her vulnerability, doesn't want to admit "it feels beyond me or that I don't know what I'm doing". If the matter is important enough, Penny says she will face it. "Eventually I knuckle down. Fortunately I'm quite bright and quite determined, and can get my resources together." For something less crucial, she simply ignores it. "If I always lose at a game I don't play that game any more."

Abby, too, has often been scared of failing; indeed, that fear overrides even the threat of extreme physical danger. She spent three years in the army, training for a crack regiment for which accepting women was an experiment. Even when in physical danger, her fear was not of falling off the cliff but of being "put on a bus and sent back to London".

A moderate fear of failure is quite usual, and can be a motivating factor: people re-double their efforts to ensure they aren't seen to fail. No one who has performed in public will have been without the flutter of nerves; some say that it is necessary for a performance to be successful. Any occasion when we are on our mettle to do well – a test, an interview – is likely to bring a similar anticipatory response.

For some, however, fear of failure produces extreme symptoms. For actors, stage fright can be paralysing, and a novelist told me: "Whenever I was working on a book, the fear of failure was on me and I was convinced I had a terminal illness." What keeps her going is an innate self-belief. "You are driven on because you have hope."

Alfie Kohn feels that

getting students to think about how they are performing also increases their fear of failure. Trying not to fail is, of course, very different from trying to succeed. One's efforts in the former case are geared at doing damage control, minimising risks, getting by… and the more emphasis teachers and parents place on performance, the more students are set back by failure (Kohn 2000, 158).

Students, he feels, don't challenge themselves: "the point is to do well, not to learn."

Fear of failure is remarkably similar to fear of success. The response to that fear might be that we don't take on a project at all or we do it in a safer, smaller way than might be possible. We are cautious; we do not take risks. Reasons can be understandable: according to a former senior civil servant, the civil service tends to be risk-averse as, if they fail, the Minister has to stand up and explain it to Parliament. It is easier to stick with the status quo, to do things in a way that we know has worked up to now. As Boyce says, fear of failure makes us do the same thing all over again. "If you do what you always do, you'll get what you always got." It leads to being stuck, which in turn can lead to a loss of morale and an inability to move on. One could say that trying to avoid failure is itself a failing mechanism.

Fear of failure is a commonplace. Its prevalence is indicated by how often we project it in our secret pleasure or open delight at the falling from grace of successful figures such as Jeffrey Archer or Jonathan Aitken, and the fallibility of celebrities. Popular culture builds people up only to knock them down. The popularity of Reality TV with its formula of public humiliation is an all too evident example, as is the regular column in the freebie newspaper, Metro: "the fickle finger of fame", delighting in the fall of former public favourites. But there is nothing new about *Schadenfreude*.

The cost of failure

Response to a failure ranges from disappointment or a mild sense of irritation at not coming up to one's own expectations to massive depression – even suicide. How we react will depend on a multitude of factors: our own general sense of ourselves; the magnitude of the failure (or how we perceive it); how we will look in others' eyes (and how much that matters); and what the impact on others will be.

As Kathryn Schulz says of making mistakes,

> They can cost us time and money, sabotage our self-confidence, and erode the trust and esteem extended to us by others. They can land us in the emergency room, or in the dog house, or in a lifetime's worth of therapy... They can hurt and humiliate us; worse, they can hurt and humiliate other people.

School and college exams are a central focus of anxiety. Coming at a particularly vulnerable time of life, for a small minority the pressure of trying to succeed can become too much, with serious consequences. Childline – the confidential 24-hour helpline in the UK – saw an increase in calls about exam stress from 600 in 2003 to 900 the following year, many from pupils worried about letting down their parents or teachers. Childline's 2011 survey showed that 96% of 1300 respondents felt anxious about exams and revision, their anxiety stemming largely from society's overblown emphasis on exam achievement as the key to lifelong success.

During a recent workshop exercise, participants were asked to explore in pairs a time when each of us had felt let down by another. My mind went back thirty years to a time when I was working on a national mass-market magazine. Newly returned to work after a seven-year break looking after my children, I was hired as a fiction journalist. Six months later I was promoted to assistant fiction editor and a year after that the fiction editor left; for six months I did both jobs. My boss, the assistant editor of the magazine, was a woman nearing retirement, a highly intelligent, experienced professional. She was also funny and warm. I liked and respected her, and knew she had a soft spot for me. She told me that she was there for me at this challenging time, and to bring any problems to her – and I did. When they appointed the new fiction editor, I did not get the job, "because I was too dependent". I felt betrayed, that I had been stood up to be knocked down, a victim of what some would call "Messianic management". I resigned on the spot, although I had to work out my three months' notice. Looking back on it, I realise that I had been naïve and had probably not understood about professional boundaries – but then, neither had she.

The immediate aftermath of such episodes is filled with emotion: anger, shame and humiliation, feeling maybe that we have let ourselves down, have not lived up to our own expectations or principles. As many have testified, it's difficult to shake off failure, and hard not to take it personally. We protect ourselves with self-justification and finding someone else to blame, in order to deny the truth of what has gone wrong. It is all too easy, after the event, to put a rosy-tinted gloss on what has happened, and if denial leads to continuing blindly along the same path, the effects can be disastrous.

The reasons for failure are often complex, and others' behaviour can be part of it, as can the dynamic between us. But, for our own soul's growth and in order to learn, maybe we need to stay with the failure, face it squarely, and see what it was in our behaviour that might have contributed to it. In the end there may be no fault, but a combination of circumstances that prevented a successful outcome. We then need to let go of our hurt, our resentment, or feeling of injustice, and move on.

In a piece of collective work, perhaps we have to accept that it was simply not to be: that, despite our processes of discernment, this was not the right project for this time and place. There may be a sadness that something we established and were deeply involved with has come to an end, maybe a sense of letting ourself or others down, but there might also be a recognition that there is a time to lay projects down, and this one had simply taken its course or had taken a wrong turning and was no longer fulfilling the needs for which it was begun.

Charles is an insolvency accountant, dealing daily with the reality of financial failure. Often the collapse has been a long time coming, with the real position a huge secret, hidden from family and colleagues. In his work, he feels that it's as if he has given his clients permission to speak, and is often assailed by a huge outpouring of failure and shame. A company is usually created by one person, and comes to feel like their child, very personal, often with the investment of years of work and thought. There is also a lifestyle to keep up: maybe private schools for the children, the golf club, a large mortgage. Losing face, Charles says, can be worse than owing £350,000 to the tax man.

Charles finds positives in his job. "A lot of our process is successful. There are always elements that can be pulled out and made to work, solutions to be found, without being naïve." And he is cheered by the resilience of the human spirit. I was surprised to hear that after "a year of hell", many business people bounce back, and often start again.

The failure of a business can, of course, have knock-on effects. A window cleaner who works in many of the pubs of London told me of the impact on the "small guys" when a company goes under. Staff can lose their jobs; subcontractors lose their money. In one recent instance, he and many others were owed money – in his case, £1500 – but he "never got a bean". In more serious cases, a "domino effect" can mean that a series of companies – or, as we have seen recently, banks – can go under. In a small community, the collapse of a company might blight the lives of the whole town. As an employer in a depressed part of England, Andy takes his responsibility very seriously. He finds having to make people redundant in hard times painful, but when it is unavoidable, he reminds himself that he has at least provided employment for many years.

When failure is unexpected, our response can be exaggerated. A young doctor told me about an incident the previous year. "A year ago I had to take a test, and didn't take it very seriously. I have so much going on in my life: a lot of hours' work, the flat, friends, hockey and so on. I failed and went to my tutor crying. He was astonished. 'Why are you crying?' 'I failed! The last time I failed was Grade 4 violin – oh, and the first time I took my driving test. How can this have happened?'" The tutor was amused at the fact that she could remember the few times she had failed and that they were so insignificant – he told her to put it in perspective and get on with her life.

The first time I remember real failure was when I was seventeen. Yes, I had had disappointments before – not getting into the secondary school of my choice, for instance, and maybe it felt terrible, but I remember seventeen as the time when I was prostrated by failure. I went to a school not renowned for its scholarly excellence. No one had applied to Oxbridge for some years and I decided not only to apply, but to apply a year early. I told everyone, and myself, that it was just a practice and that I would do it again the following year, but in my heart of hearts it didn't occur to me that I wouldn't succeed. When I did not get in, I was knocked for six, and couldn't face doing it all over again, so applied late to other universities, and scraped into my last choice.

When I was 22, and newly married, we moved to the country to be near my husband's new job. I left behind family, friends, job, all that I knew, and went to live in an idyllic little cottage. I was pregnant; I knew no one and my husband was out all day. It hadn't occurred to me that I would be miserable. I assumed I could do everything. It has taken many knocks over many years to realise – and to know in my innards – otherwise.

Susan too talked of taking success for granted. She remembers her driving test as her first failure, and remembers finding excuses and blaming others. But the major failure that she remembers was as maternity cover in an interim management position. She was meant to stay eight months, and left after only four. She remembers it as a dysfunctional organisation with a divided board, interminable bickering and politicking. She had insufficient authority and didn't know what to do. "I got out before it ruined my health." But it knocked her confidence, and it took time and several sessions with a counsellor to come to terms with the fact that she could not in fact do everything. She needed to recover in order to prevent the experience becoming a barrier to any future attempts at adventurous living.

Father James's first real sense of failure was only a few months before we spoke. A lack of communication led to him first accepting, then having to withdraw from, a new job. The experience knocked him back, leaving him with a sense of desolation, and a feeling of having let people down. But it has also made him more aware of the many disappointments in others' lives.

As Penny said, "Everyone fails. You just have to move on. I've done some stupid things. I don't like to think about it." Valerie feels she doesn't have time to fail. "I don't want to have to do things again. I don't have the time." When she failed Grade 4 violin, she went straight on to Grade 5 and passed it. "I don't think I'll ever get used to failure – I don't want to. It's also the environment you grow up in. My father would have quizzed me as to why it had happened."

Most people I have spoken to agree that every life has its share of success and failure. Failure is natural, inevitable and universal. What is important is to have a sense of balance: to have the humility not to make too much of success, the knowledge, understanding and determination to do something about failure, and maybe the wisdom to move beyond the concept of either.

5

"Fail again, fail better"
Samuel Beckett

Bankruptcy, or the failure of a company, is often the end of a business career. In Europe, particularly, it is rare for investors to consider putting money into a potential business which is to be run by someone whose former business has crashed. In the United States, there is a different view. Although it is not a given that someone who has failed will get funding, nor is failure a prerequisite for funding, investors generally look more kindly on those who have failed – as long the failure is not due to fraud or any personal wrongdoing. They consider that if a mistake has been made, it is unlikely to be made again. It is looked on as a valuable experience; a lesson has been learnt.

Scientific disciplines rely on failure as a process of elimination. Being wrong is not viewed as a negative. As Kathryn Schulz says, "As an ideal of intellectual inquiry and a strategy for the advancement of knowledge, the scientific method is essentially a monument to the utility of error." Unlike most of us, "scientists gravitate towards falsification; as a community, if not as individuals, they seek to disprove their beliefs" (32).

The most famous example is Thomas Edison, the inventor of the light bulb. When a young reporter asked him if he felt like a failure and if he thought he should just give up now, Edison is reported to have replied, "Young man, why would I feel like a failure? And why would I ever give up? I now know definitively over *9,000 ways that an electric light bulb will not work. Success is almost in my grasp." And shortly after that, and over 10,000 attempts, Edison invented the light bulb. [* Variously reported as 700 and 10,000 – but the principle is the same!]

Following the example of scientific enquiry, there is a growing culture of accepting failure as a positive contribution to the development of ideas and practice in all kinds of fields of human endeavour. Indeed, failure has suddenly become a fashionable subject. When, in spring 2010, *Time* magazine listed ten important trends for the new decade, it put at number six: "in defence of failure". Celebrities and billionaire businessmen from Alan Sugar to Morten Lund have been falling over themselves to confess their failures – and explain how they overcame them to rise to even greater heights.

Over the last few years there have been several initiatives on both sides of the Atlantic exploring the nature of failure and some of its positive aspects. In 2008, the UK Royal Society for the encouragement of arts, manufactures and commerce (RSA) invited Fellows to explore the subject, and a year later hosted the first Failure Colloquium. It was from this that the "Glory of Failure" project and *The Failure Files* were born.

In the USA, Penn State's College of Engineering runs a course called Failure 101. Its director, Jack Matson, stresses the connection between creativity and risk, teaching people to unlearn years of practising risk aversion. "No issue is more important to the engineer or entrepreneur than intelligent failure," says Matson. Another example is the Howard Hughes Medical Institute, which "has an 'investigator' programme which explicitly urges 'researchers to take risks, to explore unproven avenues, to embrace the unknown – even if it means uncertainty or the chance of failure'" (Harford, 101). In his book, *Adapt: Why Success Always Starts with Failure,* Tim Harford shows how the world's most complex and important problems – including terrorism, climate change, poverty, innovation, and the financial crisis – can only be solved by rapid experimenting and adaptation (Amazon). His lessons are: "First, try new things, expecting that some will fail. Second, make failure survivable: create safe spaces for failure or move forward in small steps... And third, make sure you know when you've failed. Or you will never learn" (224). Some corporations, including Google, have got the message.

Recognising that "in the real world things go wrong or do not work out as planned", Donna Leat called for "stories of things that 'go wrong'" (22). As if in answer, early in 2011, Engineers Without Borders launched a website, www.admittingfailure .com, making a bold challenge to development charities across Canada and around the world: stop fearing failure, start innovating, start an honest conversation about mistakes. Along with the website, EWB released their *2011 Failure Report*. The need to be open about and share mistakes and failure is summarised by Ian Smillie in its conclusion:

> The development business is largely uncharted territory. If we knew how to end poverty, we would have done it a long time ago. And yet the enterprise is notoriously risk-averse; donors demand results and punish failure. The development challenge is not to avoid the risk that comes with charting new paths. It is not to deny failure. It is to learn, to remember, and to apply what is being remembered.

As we have seen earlier, it is important to move beyond evaluation and performance measurement. Part of that progression is to accept the contribution of mistakes: to recognise how important it is to create a culture in every field where feedback matters and failure is possible.

In his lecture at the 2010 Free Thinking festival, entitled, "The Joys of Failure", screenwriter Frank Cottrell Boyce speaks eloquently of the place of failure in the process of innovation.

Failure, he says, can be success in waiting/in the making, part of a work in progress. What you are doing may be the best you can do for the moment, and will give some breathing space. It all takes time. If success comes after years of trying/failure, you know what you're dealing with, you're ready. It may come as a moment of inspiration after long dry periods. We need to learn to live with our failure and see how it can work for us.

In the eyes of the world success is nearly always what we had before, but a little bit better... We can succeed at what we have imagined. Surely we should be reaching out for what we could never have imagined. That can only come about if we are alert to the accidental, to the grace of chaos.

We need to be open to failure, Boyce says, as "the loam on which ideas are born". "Wisdom is what you get when you don't get what you want." "If an environment is created where it is OK to fail, amazing things can happen". Columbus didn't get to India, "but it was still worth the trip". As a friend said, success can come when you are least expecting it. "Something happens to a person after a period of time has elapsed from a failed venture, and a successful outcome occurs."

Mark was in the entertainment business for nearly forty years. He feels he has made thousands of mistakes, and is content with that. "I'm preparing for my next mistake." As a magician, he understood that facing your mistakes, learning to love them, is the only way to get things right. He says that the nearest to perfection that he has got to is as a magician: by failing again and again and again, *and in front of people.*

Physicist Fritjof Capra feels that there are misunderstandings about the nature of scientific research. It is not about rejecting the earlier versions, but about building on them.

When theories or models are improved in successive steps, the knowledge does not change in an arbitrary way. Each new theory will be related to the preceding one in a well-defined way, although in a scientific revolution this may not be apparent for a long time. The new theory does not invalidate the old one in an absolute way; it merely improves the approximation. For example, quantum physics did not show that Newtonian mechanics is wrong; it merely showed that Newtonian physics is limited (370).

Designer and artist Matt Soar gives more details of how failure can help in the creative process in his blog, "Failing Again: A Routine and Necessary Part of Creative Practice":

We should perhaps openly embrace failure rather than assiduously avoiding it.

From our earliest days in school many of us are encouraged to court failure; to learn by our mistakes. Nancy Skolos remembers that one of her teachers used to say, "A good failure is worth a lot of mediocre successes." To varying degrees, we carry this sensibility through into professional practice. For example, Jonathan Hoefler says, "Increasingly I think about the work that I do not so much as a directed effort, but as the ability to recognize accidents and interpret them productively. Even failures have their place, since without them there's no progress: anything that's truly 'experimental' has to run the risk of failure." Hoefler describes these moments as "happy accidents": "Several times a day, some misstep on the computer produces an unexpected result, and sometimes these results are fetching, intriguing, even provocative."
http://observatory.designobserver.com/entry.html?entry=6627)

Barry Crisp urges us to come clean.

Just what is it about admitting failure that turns us from sitting on the shoulders of giants to silent snails at a mere shudder of the thought of failure? Many people, especially social entrepreneurs, fail to share or execute on their ideas because the failure associated with innovation may not be rewarded in development. By hiding our failures, we are condemning ourselves to repeat them and we are stifling innovation. In doing so, we are condemning ourselves to continue under-performance in across [*sic*] all sectors.

Barry Crisp, http://i-genius.org/news/index.php/id/273

Conversely, as he says, "by admitting our failures – publicly sharing them not as shameful acts, but as important lessons – we contribute to a culture in development where failure is recognised as essential to success."

Even if evidence of the positive impact of failure is persuasive, no one can pretend that it doesn't hurt. Facing the reality, which may dent our pride or even mean the loss not only of our status or good name, but considerable sums of money – our own or others' – is painful. And if lessons are to be learnt, it may take time. A venture capitalist told me that when a start-up funded by investors' money went under, it took him five years to work through the experience mentally until he was confident that he would not repeat the same mistakes. During that time he returned to college to gain new skills.

Although there is an honourable history and a groundswell of recent support for the positive influence of failure, there is a long way to go. As a young doctor told me, in medical journals all the attention is on the cases that made a difference, not on the thousands that didn't, even if they saved millions of pounds. There are no prizes for them.

Failure as entertainment

What Kathryn Schulz calls the "mismatch between expectation and reality" has provided a rich seam for what is known as the incongruity theory of humour. Laughing at misfortune and botched attempts to succeed is an ancient tradition.

The nature of the comedian Tommy Cooper's performance was to make an art out of public failure. His stage act generally consisted of failed magic tricks – occasionally throwing in one that worked when least expected. The theatre critic Ken Tynan said of him that he was "convulsed by his own incompetence" and that he demonstrated "the futility of human effort". It is sad to read that his acts mirrored his own sense of self. Even after thirty years at the top of his profession, he was apparently plagued by self-doubt. He didn't think he was funny, and imagined that his success might disappear at any moment.

Another example of an entertainer who put failure at the centre of his art was the director and actor Jacques Tati, who created the accident-prone Monsieur Hulot: "An inoffensive, ordinary-looking middle-aged man, he unwittingly sets off a series of disasters wherever he goes and then saunters away, totally oblivious to the mayhem he has caused" (http://filmsde-france.com/FDF_jtati.html). Tati shows that the use of failure as a comic device can be inoffensive and kind – a million miles from the cruel public humiliation at the centre of such programmes as Big Brother.

Central to this tradition of failure entertainment is the ancient art of clowning. Clowns, too, tap into our fear of failure by acts showing them trying very hard but never succeeding. As the "Holy Fool", Roly Bain, has written, "the clown reminds us that we're allowed to fail, that we can learn from failure, laugh at failure and move on...In a society that is geared to success at all costs, the clown is a necessary counterbalance." http://www.hospitalclown.com/)

Clowns ... are losers with a winner's soul, they stubbornly go through countless ordeals until they find their own solution within the confusion of their problems.

By taking a step to the side, clowning shows us how vain, derisory and hopeless are the efforts towards success. It is through failure that clowns show their wisdom. http://www.nosetonose.info/articles/bertilarticle.htm

"Fail again, fail better"

And it is only in self-acceptance, in admitting failure, that it works.

In my fifties, I did two terms of evening classes on clowning, and it was transformative. I learnt to play. I learnt to be less goal-directed, to be in the present, to value innocence and silence. A friend told me of a clowning course she had been on, where the teacher asked them to prepare a solo show to perform in front of the other students. "I'm going to fail you all," he warned. Despite the warning, the participants did not really believe him, and worked at their performances, trying to make them as good as they could be. When in due course they were failed, Frances says it was a really useful lesson about failure. "The sky did not fall in," she says. We do not have to fear failure; we can survive.

There is no shortage of failed public performances in such shows as Britain's Got Talent, and indeed karaoke in every town. Giving an opportunity to everyone to perform can be painful. It's only when something is created with the chutzpah and self-awareness of, for instance, the Really Terrible Orchestra, that it turns an uncomfortable experience into an enjoyable one.

> Five-star the RTO continues to lead the revolution for the musically disadvantaged with its unique musical interpretations. A triumph that proves bad is good. With its blend of humour, musicality and lack of technical prowess, the players surge through a lively programme taking the audience with them, creating a wave of excitement and hope that nothing will go wrong. The RTO never disappoints. (website)

Despite the self-mockery of its name, there is a seriousness of intent to enjoy playing music. You have to be quite good to be bad.

Florence Foster Jenkins was an American soprano who became famous for her complete lack of rhythm, pitch and tone. But the difference was that she was unintentionally funny. She really thought she could sing.

Acceptance

As we saw in an earlier chapter, the usual response to failure is often blame of others or of self, and a growing sense of inadequacy. A better response is to see a rejection or a failure to achieve as a form of guidance, an indicator that one has taken a wrong turning. On several occasions in recent years, while feeling around for what to do next, I have applied for jobs or scholarships that I didn't get. With hindsight, I can see that that was just as well. My life took quite another turning. These days, even at the moment of rejection, although disappointed, I can accept that it wasn't to be. "OK, so it's not that, but something else." The challenge is to wait until clarity is reached.

6

Being a failure

Taking an external view of failure in our projects may enable us to see the lurking success; patience, resilience and flexibility of approach may lead to more positive outcomes. But from the inside, and in our personal lives, it is a different matter. We take failure seriously; it dents our self-esteem, or may confirm the lack of it; it's hard to leave it behind. We have a tendency to dwell on what has not gone well, on criticism, on a few bad reviews, even if most have been good. An entertainer said that he had got a few bad reviews over the years. "They confirm your worst fears. Not a huge surprise." Marshall Rosenberg mentions a workshop that he ran with more than a hundred participants, "all of whom had evaluated it very highly, with the exception of one person". What lingered in his mind "was that one person's dissatisfaction" (191). A woman I interviewed said, "The moment you stand up to do anything, you feel that it is you, and the moment someone rejects it, you feel they are rejecting you." She talked of a successful painter friend of hers who had just had a couple of paintings turned down by an exhibition. Despite her success, it knocked her back to doubting herself. "The work hadn't changed at all," her friend said. "Only she had changed."

We need to be affirmed, for our egos to be stroked. Self-esteem is frequently precarious; fear of failure never far from the surface. Some people don't even believe compliments or affirmations when they are given. Receiving parental disapproval as a child injects a negative sense of self that is hard to change.

If success is characterised by being largely external and short-lived, failure digs deep into the human psyche and, if we are not careful, can dwell there. If success belongs mainly to others, failure is deeply personal, attacking our perceptions of self-worth. When I asked Rob about failure, he became serious. "Oh, that's a real emotion, where you get hurt. Despairing. How you perceive yourself. Poor self-esteem. Not much worse than that, is there? 'Abandon hope all you that enter here.'"

There is an ocean of difference between an occasional lack of success, and feeling a failure. Identifying oneself as a failure means that whatever we do will not feel enough. Such a hard-wired view of self is usually imposed in childhood and, no matter how much is achieved in later life, no matter how much love and support is given by partners or affirmation given by colleagues, it is unlikely to change. Disapproval, constant criticism or abuse of a child confirms his own view of himself in later life. Without receiving loving acceptance as a child, it is almost impossible to think well of ourselves. Failure becomes a familiar companion. A mental health chaplain put her finger on it, when she mentioned that the problem with many of her clients was a lack of resilience. She mentioned a friend who "sets himself up for failure". There's an expectation that whatever he does will not succeed.

Low achievement and low self-esteem form a vicious circle. Low achievement can beget low self-esteem and vice versa. Being told by parents or teachers that you are good for nothing can become a self-fulfilling prophecy. Even if someone reacts to such a prophecy by feeling driven to achieve success in career or monetary terms, the sense of failure can still be ingrained. Nothing is good enough. It was sobering to discover what a large percentage of the people I talked to are still swayed by childhood experience and parental influence.

Mark quoted from Orwell's essay, "Benefit of Clergy": "Autobiography is only to be trusted when it reveals something disgraceful. A man who gives a good account of himself is probably lying, since any life when viewed from the inside is simply a series of defeats." Mark said that he has always felt it to be true. He felt that he had a similar experience to Orwell at boarding school, in being

taught how to be a success by having all your failures exposed. I see my life from inside as a series of failures. That's because I had a sense of what success would be. I was probably thought more successful than I thought I was. I'm hard on myself.

Mark has spent years in therapy but it changed nothing. His father was hard on himself, and he and his mother were hard on each other and on him. "Can one inherit being hard on oneself? I'd find it hard to call anything of mine a success. I'd always spot what was unsuccessful about it."

When Barbara, now in middle age, left a senior job in the corporate sector after fifteen years to move into the voluntary sector, it was a high-risk strategy that she knew would be opposed by her parents whose successful lives and traditional attitudes have cast a heavy shadow on her life.

My parents are incredibly successful – have achieved everything they set out to do. They have a formulaic approach, believing in hard work, consistency. They achieved in everything except with their four children who didn't turn into the people they wanted them to be. They are always interrogating: "What did you do this week? And what did they say?" It's the opposite of nurturing. Can't discuss anything without being judged or criticised.

Being criticised, she says is a "physical pain". She has never had a thick skin. We spent almost as long discussing her parents' views on success as her own. Thinking of her achievements over many years, I said, "I'm surprised you care". Her response was: "You haven't met them." Margaret, referring to parents who are long-dead, said, "I know just what she means". Even beyond the grave, the shadow of parental disapproval can fall heavily on present lives.

Andy's family history is one of extremes of success and failure. His father has been "very successful": he is still alive at 87, still married; he had a "good war", and afterwards success in the City. Andy's mother's family, on the other hand, lost everything in the depression in the 1930s: home, everything. There was not even enough to feed the children, who were put into foster care. Andy's first memory of his own sense of failure was that he was not good enough for his father; he was not, for instance, good at sport. As one of his friends once shrewdly commented, "Of course you've always felt you're a failure." And, despite having a good deal of money and several properties, that is what he does feel, both in business and personally. Living in London reinforces that sense, he says: he is no longer a big fish in a small sea. Although he acknowledges that in some areas he has been a success, Andy says he has to stand outside himself to see it. He tries to look objectively but feels he is making up stories to try to make himself feel better.

William started our discussion by saying, "I see myself as a failure." He went on to tell me how at the age of seven he was diagnosed with asthma, followed by a life beset by illness and periods of depression. As a child, he was physically removed and lonely. He was not able to play sport, never learnt to play football, and as a result hates the whole culture. At seven too he decided that he was an atheist, and that he did not want to get married – and in his late forties he has not changed his mind. He told me candidly that he has also had periods of mania, and has spent years in therapy.

William also talked a good deal about his parents, who had high expectations for him (his father has a PhD). He himself left school at 16 with four poor O levels, and had no wish to continue with academic education. When he walked out of an engineering course at college a year later, it caused a furious row at home, after which he packed his bags and left, making himself homeless at the age of seventeen. He spent the first night on a park bench, then went to stay with friends. After getting a job as a labourer, earning £40 per week, he was able to afford a bedsit at £7.50. Apart from occasional spells of temporary work, William has not been able to hold down a job and, for most of his adult life (since 1983) has been living on benefits and hand-outs from his parents. Despite later academic achievements and a considerable contribution to a local neighbourhood association, his lack of economic independence weighs heavily on him.

My father too regarded himself as a failure. A brilliant pupil, he gained an open scholarship to Oxford at the age of 16, was a high flyer in public service, and broke down in his thirties. Diagnosed with schizophrenia, he worked only briefly afterwards and spent most of the next forty years in and out of mental hospitals. In the early years of his illness, he acquired a profound faith, coming to Catholicism and feeling called to a monastic life, to which he was not admitted because of his mental history, and because he had a wife living. But he prayed and read, amassing cuttings from a wide variety of faiths that I discovered after his death. It was after his death too that I realised that he had attained a purity of spirit unimaginable during his earlier career-driven life. My father suffered greatly during his life, considering himself a Job, but to call him a failure would be to negate both his struggles and his profound insights.

When I told someone that I had always felt an outsider, she wisely responded: "Have you ever met anyone who felt an 'insider'?" As I said, I have met few people who think of themselves as successful. I don't think this is because they feel failures – that is generally all too obvious – but simply that they don't notice. Success and failure don't enter into the equation. Charles, for instance, never thinks of what he does in those terms. Although he could see, objectively, that coming from a council house in New Zealand to become a partner in a large firm of London accountants might be classed as "success", he found it an artificial concept, not how he thinks of his life. Most of us do what we do, and the question of judging it doesn't often come into our minds.

Failure, like poverty (and of course poverty is an example of the world's view of failure, as well as an example of its own failure to balance available resources) is, in affluent countries at least, largely hidden. We generally talk positively about what we do – if not actually bragging about success, giving off a general air of it. Failure we generally keep to ourselves. Like any sales person, my years as a literary agent taught me to put a positive gloss on everything I was selling. Everything I said was truthful, but I kept the negatives to myself. So it is for most of us most of the time in talking about our own lives.

Some feelings of failure come from the sense that we are not living our life fully. Although the notion that we only use 10% of our brain cells is a myth (all of our highly complex brains have a function though not all of it may be firing at the same time), it is certainly true that most people do not fulfil the full extent of their potential. I was told of a dying man who confessed to feeling a failure because he knew that he had a vocation, but had not been able to find it, and I can never forget the furious passion with which a friend turned on me to say: "You don't know how it feels to want to have faith, and not have it."

Charles's sense of failure came from the secret knowledge during the years he lived with a wife and two teenage daughters that he was gay. By putting his energy into work, he tried to turn failure in one part of his life into success in another. As a result, he thinks that others mistook his overcompensation for ambition. Charles came out a couple of years ago, and now lives with a male partner. Since admitting his real sexuality, he says, the sense of failure has retreated but has been replaced with guilt at leaving his wife, although they are once again on good terms. Being true to himself, he says, has resulted in an increased creativity in all he does.

A public figure with high achievements and a broad range of fulfilling activities well into his sixties is still not content. When I asked whether there was anything in life that he'd still like to achieve, his response was that, even after three attempts, "I haven't managed a happy marriage."

Raymond is seventeen and at school in London. He grew up in Malaysia, living with his mother until he moved to the UK a couple of years ago to live with his father. Half-white, half-Malaysian, he felt that he didn't fit in anywhere. "One of my biggest failures", he said, "is I could have studied harder. I let them push me down. Others in Malaysia were very racist. I let it affect me. I let myself down because I let things get to me." Raymond described himself as emotionally fragile, vulnerable. His biggest failure, he says, is time management, partly because he cannot bear to leave home until he feels he looks OK. He dislikes this aspect of himself, but feels that a lot of people – most people – judge by appearance.

Indeed, to the extent that it is an external evaluation, the concept of success is entirely about how we appear to ourselves and to others. We need to look good in our world, whatever that is. Worrying about what others think is a common enough problem, although most of us would not go so far as to consider a lack of social poise as failure. But in some circles social embarrassment is crippling. The designer Barbara Amiel said that she felt that she and her husband Conrad Black were failures because when they left a party they admitted they had to use public transport, not a private jet. A banker said that if he earned less than £150,000 a year he would feel "ashamed, a failure". One man I talked to spoke of his partner being "continually embarrassed by the fact that we do not own our own London property and sees renting as failure despite my comfortably being able to pay over £500 a week rent. Because it bugs him so much I keep thinking that I am a failure in not providing us with a proper home."

A friend (also Barbara) told me: "A couple of weeks ago [the end of 2010] I had the most horrible look in the mirror and thought what have I achieved in the last year – zilch." But she did finish the enormous project of refurbishing and moving into her very beautiful flat, which she says has been a healing project. "A flat doesn't talk to you, doesn't tell you you're useless." In the previous eighteen months she had been living in a "minute soulless beige box" doing nothing except sorting out the building and writing funding applications that failed.

This came after a period of what she regards as three failures and a decreasing ability to trust, feeling that what she learnt from the last of the failures was about mental health (which she later felt was better described as self-esteem).

What does mental health look like? For me it looks like a series of layers. When all is going well the strata are strong. When my confidence is shaken, it doesn't show on the topsoil but in the bottom layers, there's a tsunami bubbling up. The way you wake up in the morning, the state of mind affects how you respond when someone says they can't make lunch and doesn't suggest another date. When you're shaken you don't know whom to trust.

7

"There is a crack in everything"

In a Navajo rug there is always an imperfection woven into the corner. And interestingly enough, it's where "the Spirit moves in and out of the rug"... Perfection is not the elimination of imperfection. That's our Western either/or, need-to-control thinking. Perfection, rather, is the ability to incorporate imperfection! (Richard Rohr, quoted in Townsend, 53)

We saw in Chapter 5 that mistakes and shortcomings in our work and in our personal lives can not only be overcome, but can provide necessary stepping stones to a more productive outcome. If squarely faced, failure can be a necessary part of success, a positive contribution to life. But in the previous chapter we saw the devastating and lasting effects of *feeling* a failure. To take a positive view of this state is certainly challenging – and yet, at a profound level suited to the depth of despair, it is indeed possible. Let us dive in.

George Orwell believed that it was impossible to combine social success with a religious belief. Certainly Christian teaching (apart from that of the "Prosperity" or "Success" gospel of some American evangelical churches) subverts any notion of worldly success. Jesus' teaching – and indeed his life, as we see it in the Gospels – turns any concept of social success on its head. As an Anglican priest said in his sermon recently, "What is success? Jesus only had two followers when he was on the cross: his mother and his best friend." The picture of leadership and kingship that emerges from the New Testament is the contrary of what was expected in his day, or indeed of what we expect in our own. It is difficult to fully understand how revolutionary it was and is. We find it no easier now to believe that it is the meek who will inherit the earth, or that the poor in spirit or those persecuted for righteousness' sake will be the ones to enter the kingdom of heaven. This is still unlike any kingdom that we know on earth.

It is not only in Christianity that we find such a paradoxical concept. Consider the following, from the *Tao Te Ching*, written in about the fourth century BC:

> Therefore, desiring to rule over the people,
> One must in one's words humble oneself before them;
> And, desiring to lead the people,
> One must, in one's person, follow behind them. (Tzu, 128)

Or, as we read in Matthew (KJV, 20:16): "The first shall be last and the last first." The picture we have of Jesus is of someone who devotes his attention to those – the outsiders and failures: the prostitutes and tax gatherers – who were widely regarded as "the last". Parables about the Prodigal Son or the lost sheep are about failure. It is those who have gone under who need help. "It is not the healthy who need a doctor," said Jesus, "but the sick. I have come to call not the righteous, but sinners" (Mark 2:15-17 NIV).

Paradoxical and counter-cultural these teachings may be, but – often to our surprise – most of us, believers or not, have experienced their truth.

Without direct experience of Jesus' paradoxical scenarios, they would appear on the surface to be foolish indeed. However, immunity to their promises usually doesn't last long. At some point, life gives us the opportunity to choose either logic, retribution and legal justice or acceptance, forgiveness, and the "other cheek." Nearly every day there are opportunities to practise the opposite of the acceptable norms in reactions, thoughts, ideas, attitudes and actions.

Jesus' paradoxical position endeavors the release of truth

in its perfection; a truth that shows us that nobility of soul is what is truly imperial, that realized humility is indeed palatial and that love links us with the universal nature and eternal power of God. (Lucinda Vardey, www.dallaluce.com)

It is not just that those who have "sinned" or failed are in more need; they are also more open to what he has to say. We know from experience that failure is painful. We have seen in Chapter 5 that, if received constructively, it can also help us reconsider our projects, and make necessary adjustments. At a more profound level, utter failure, dark times, trauma, can challenge us in more significant ways, can open us to change not just in our outward actions, but in our very selves.

It took me a long time to understand that many Biblical texts, in both Old and New Testaments, are not judgements – "God decrees that it shall be so" – but reflections of reality. It *is* so, that is how it is. It is in our meekness, our poverty of spirit, our brokenness, that blessing will come. It is inherent in these states of being that we are more open, more likely to find reality or "the kingdom of heaven". When we are bolstered with our own sense of importance, status and success, we are armoured; our ears are shut.

The experience of brokenness is simply a fact of life for us all…Consider some of the following sayings and ask yourself whether you have ever used any of them with reference to your own life: broken promise, broken heart, damaged relationship, bruised ego, shattered dream… The irony is that you are more likely to catch a glimpse of your inner beauty when you DO fail at achieving your external goals. You may well get low and enter a symbolic desert for a while, but the desert is the place where you will find your divine self. You see, in such places there is no way you can rely on your achievements or goals; all you have is what you are. Naked, empty, powerless – and staying with that human emptiness WILL bring you into contact with your true inner treasure. (Townsend, 20, 38)

It is not without significance that it is at times of failure and brokenness that we become able to see another dimension, open ourselves up to faith. It was so in my own life, and I know it had nothing to do with escapism. It was a tough, and irresistible, call. It was brokenness. It was what it took to be cracked open to access another dimension. It's a perspective that is most vividly expressed in the Leonard Cohen song, "There is a crack in every-thing. That's how the light gets in." And by many religious teachers, including the Franciscan Richard Rohr, who says that "failures and humiliation open up the heart space".

Jean Vanier, founder of the L'Arche communities where people of different abilities live alongside each other, talked of the time when he was called to come and work with a young man with severe disabilities. He found it hard, but learnt that that was where he had to be.

I suddenly realized that ...God wanted to dwell in his broken person so that He could speak from that vulnerability into the world of strength, and call people to become vulnerable (from a talk "Journey to L'Arche", first broadcast on 1 October 1989).

Making ourselves vulnerable includes letting go of certainty, and opening ourselves to the rigors of doubt. We are accustomed to being clear, being sure, and being right. Inner whispers that tell us otherwise are easier to ignore. Even if we are intellectually aware that others may not agree, certainty is an attractive position and bolsters our confidence. In comparison, doubt is dangerous: akin to failure in its potential to undermine firmly held convictions and precious beliefs, including about ourselves.

We need to let go of the quest for individual perfection,

forgive our weaknesses, and accept what is. In fact, someone who exudes success and apparent invincibility is not attractive. When we admit that we don't have all the answers, others feel as if they might have something to offer. One of the best-loved aphorisms of the Religious Society of Friends (Quakers) is: "Think it possible that you may be mistaken." When we admit our mistakes and our vulnerability we are more lovable, both by God and by other people. We have opened ourselves up to a shared understanding of need, and to the possibility of mutual healing. According to Matthew Fox, "it is in fact our imperfections that most unite us and make us a social organism whose parts are busy assisting one another. For it is shared weakness and need that draws from a group its gifts and powers of healing" (111). As the Tao says, "Weakness is the means the way employs" (Tzu, 25).

> A man is supple and weak when living, but hard and stiff when dead. Grass and trees are pliant and fragile when living, but dried and shrivelled when dead. Thus the hard and the strong are the comrades of death; the supple and the weak are the comrades of life. (*ibid.*, 138)

In my case, the light that came through the crack included an understanding of a new way of being, a letting go of the need to try to control what happened in my life. Instead of an ambitious drive to make things happen, I knew now that I would be led. Without any idea of what I would do, I sold the business I had run for the past fourteen years, and waited. I did not have to wait long for another door to open. Trust had come into the equation.

A priest told me of his imminent move from a large team parish to another parish where he will be working more on his own. He has been asked if it is a promotion. He wondered what that meant. He wouldn't get more money – all the clergy are paid the same stipend – and he is unlikely to be living in a house as lovely as his current one. He sees the need for development in his work, and to keep his ministry fresh, but he feels there is an unhealthy strand in the Church of England of "progression" and "career-mindedness". "We don't have the infrastructure for that." With about 12,000 priests and only 150 bishops in the UK, if every priest wanted to be a bishop, there would be a lot of disappointment.

A Catholic friend told me a tale of two bishops. One, it seemed, could be spotted as a potential bishop, even at seminary. The other, when offered the post, felt that that was his cross. The honour and all those responsibilities would pull him into the world; he feared they would impede his spiritual journey. In the spiritual realm, ambition can be dangerous.

8

Transformation: some stories

Sean is a young man who has spent time in a young offenders' institution. At this low point in his life, he took part in a workshop of the Alternatives to Violence Project, which explores ways of dealing with conflict – a natural part of any life. One of the fundamental building blocks of this programme is affirmation, and an exercise often run at the end of workshops is one called "Affirmation posters". Everyone is asked to put a sheet of paper on their chair with their name on it, then all walk round the room, writing comments on each other's posters. Only positive and truthful comments may be made.

At the end of this exercise, Sean looked at his poster, and was visibly moved. "Oh," he said, "no one's written anything nice about me since I was about five. Can I take it home to my Mum?" Two of the facilitators at that session, talking about it some time later, mentioned Sean. "I'd love to know what happened to him," said one. "Oh," said the other, "I know what happened to him. He became a youth worker."

I have done some work in prisons, including spending several days with a group of men serving life sentences. I did not know their specific offences, but knew that most were likely to have killed. Many had been in prison for a very long time and had worked on themselves to a considerable degree. I was humbled by the wisdom in the room. Some will never be released; others, now given indeterminate sentences, are long past their original tariffs. Day in, day out, they are reminded of their criminal behaviour; it is hard for them to believe that they have done, or indeed are, anything else. I turned, as I said goodbye, and said: "Remember, you are not your offence". And we are not our failures (or indeed, our achievements).

Transformations such as these occur on a daily basis – but not without huge personal effort, or pain. A friend of mine sent me her own story, and wondered if I would like it as an example of success. It is an example of success in overcoming adversity, of acknowledging the reality of who she is. Anne is bi-polar, though it took her long time to acknowledge it. She wanted to become a guinea pig to help research, and finally has been asked to take part in a study to find out how the brain changes in adulthood, and how it's possible to age healthily.

> Quite recently I have been able to own that I too am a victim of this illness and it has made all the difference to know and trace, even into childhood, areas of extreme sensitivity – thirteen places I could have named "home", up to the age of 23, and fourteen school changes up to the age of 16.
>
> I have not tried to hide the shame and stigma which mental illness brings, but I have not been overtly enthusiastic about talking at length on the subject. And I do wonder how I survived. Despite the trauma, despite the words "nervous breakdown" masking the true nature of what has happened, I think I am a survivor. And strongly characterised, having had long episodes of health between episodes of illness.

Anne offers "boundless apologies for being the source of anxiety and even wrathful fed-upness. I don't know how else I can say sorry. I cannot also say I will never be ill again."

A permanent state cannot be assured. Clients of Alcoholics Anonymous programmes never talk of cure, but of being "recovering alcoholics". A tendency to mental illness and addiction is there for life.

* * *

Joseph was brought up in Glasgow in a Catholic family He was the eldest of twelve children. "I do not think my folk had any great aspirations for their number one son. My difficulty is that I do not have great memory recall, although I do remember walking out the school gate with my dad and him asking me whether I was sure that I wanted to leave school at 15 to which I answered most certainly yes."

In 2000, Joseph was sent to prison for something he didn't do. He served 19 months of a 3½ year sentence. "When I was convicted, I thought I can either get bitter and twisted about this, or think of the positive aspects. That sent me on a journey and I've never looked back. I'm not how I was before." The biggest positive, he says, was giving up smoking four days into his sentence. He'd been smoking for forty years. He became more assertive and, he says, also more chilled out. When a friend visited him in prison, having been used to seeing him with a phone to each ear, working all the hours that God sent, he found him in a much more relaxed state. While in prison Joseph admitted to himself that his marriage of some 35 years was over, and had been over for some time. When we spoke he was still living under the same roof as his ex-wife, but was in a new relationship, and was buying a narrow boat as a new independent home. He has now divorced and is living on the boat.

A couple of years after coming out of prison, Joseph became a prison visitor and, having himself been inside, gained a good deal of street cred with those he talked to. He has been working with an organisation called Circles of Support and Accountability for about four years, as one of a group supporting sex offenders on release, "to prevent the next victim". The group not only helps the former offender to re-enter normal life, but guarantees to contact the authorities if their client shows any sign of re-offending. Joseph has worked with four clients, and is still in touch with the first one. He is also a trustee for a homeless charity. Many of the people he works with have low self-esteem, and he is able to talk to them from a place of experience and understanding.

Joseph is working as before in the freight business, but whereas he used to be ambitious, always looking for success, he now lives in the moment.

I have a noticeably different outlook, to my work, my work colleagues and the environment. Mainly that I am comfortable with myself, the consequence of which is that when I come across injustices: racism, bullying etc., I am more than likely to get on their case which I am not sure I would have done before. My ex has noticed a difference and she thinks I am weird. I am my own person.

Suffering, adversity, failure are agents of change or even transformation. A sense of failure can jolt us into a new life, or simply enable us to make the necessary adjustment to make our old life work.

9

Setting goals

If you want to make God laugh, make a plan.

We live much of our lives in the future tense. We plan what we will do tomorrow or after work today. We write "to do" lists, make resolutions for the New Year. We plan where our children (sometimes as yet unborn) will go to school. We have diaries full of future engagements, some in a year's time. In business, there are five-year plans, and staff appraisals asking: "Where do you see yourself in three years' time?"

We have plans, intentions, ambitions – and goals. A goal has a more definite quality than a plan: it's an endpoint – the word has another meaning, after all, as a physical entity. To set a goal is to define parameters for our planning, to set up an expectation of outcomes, with the consequent possibilities of success or failure. As Abby, a project manager, said, "If you don't have targets and goals, how can you have success and failure?" She's always had goals, says that's how she lives her life. "I can't not have them." As the youngest of four children, with big age-differences between her and the others, she sometimes felt invisible, and thinks now that that might have something to do with the fact that she has always felt the need to set and meet challenges in her life.

Increasingly, how-to books define success as achieving one's goals, whatever they might be. Kelly Holmes, who said that "at age 14 I wanted to join the army and be an Olympic champion. I've managed both", gives six steps for others to take to achieve their goals. In *The Success Principles*, Jack Canfield and Janet Switzer suggest ten steps to learn how to "take responsibility for your life, set goals and manage time, invest in developing knowledge and core skills, face up to what isn't working and stay motivated, focus on your unique abilities, transcend other peoples limiting opinions" – and more. "Decide what you want," they say, "believe you deserve it and practise the principles, and with these powerful new habits you can experience astonishing opportunities and extraordinary results in all aspects of your life, from your career to your relationships" (Amazon). Life courses also often ask participants to set goals for themselves – think of where you'd like to be in six months' time, a year, five years.

I'm embarrassed to remember just how goal-centred I used to be, even as a child. We didn't call them goals at the time, but I had clear aims and worked to achieve them. As a schoolgirl, I used to clown around in class, entertaining my fellow pupils but, deciding that I wanted to be head girl, I stopped messing about in time for that to happen. As a teenager, I set myself lists of books that I "ought" to have read, and read them. At 12, I read the Bible, a chapter a night (including all the "begats"). After having my own children, I wanted to be back at work by the age of thirty (and just managed it). In my thirties, I wrote a novel, sitting down each day to write. I finished it; I wanted to have written a novel – but I had nothing to say, and it was an empty shell. I had missed the mark. Despite succeeding in my quantifiable goal, in any meaningful sense I had failed.

Goals are often an indication of dissatisfaction. If we were content in the present, goals would be unnecessary – and so perhaps it is natural that we are keener on setting goals when most of our life lies ahead, or at a time later in life when we consider what we have (and haven't) achieved, or when we face a turning-point in our lives.

Penny described how she and a group of friends responded to one such turning point – coming up to their thirtieth birthdays. One of the men was thoroughly depressed. He had set himself a plan for what he expected to have achieved by the age of thirty but most of his expectations had not been met – he hadn't married, and wasn't on a set career path. Others who didn't attach so much importance to the milestone weren't so bothered by what they had and hadn't achieved. Penny also spoke of a couple she knew who had made a seven-year plan for their relationship. When one of them wanted to do something different, the relationship broke up. Again, expectations had not been met, and it was hard to cope with that. Penny herself describes herself as a doer and a planner but says she doesn't set goals. She has a sense of direction but doesn't feel "I must be there by then."

Having concentrated a good deal on letting go of my own goal-directed thinking, I was brought up short by two friends who stressed the importance of goals. One is a trainee priest; the other a poet and painter, so their emphasis was unexpected. For Fiona, who grew up in a household with no rules, finding a structure for her life and work is essential. She needs a container, she says, and indeed, collects empty containers – boxes, tins, and baskets – physical representations of an inner need: "I have to have goals," she says, "otherwise I'd never do anything." With her housemate, she is working on a specific goal-setting programme, based on the book, *Your Best Year Yet* by Jinny Ditzler. It is, Fiona says, a long process, beginning with looking at the previous year: its disappointments, successes, what you tell yourself about it, and what that is really saying. You then write the opposite version of that – so if you are telling yourself that you are rubbish, you might write down, "I am capable of all that I would like to do." You look at the roles you have in your life, and your values. Only then do you write down your goals for the next year, connected to the roles you have. If you are not achieving something you set yourself, but the role is an unimportant one – Fiona cited riding her bicycle – you look at why that is happening, then let yourself off the hook. If the role is one that is important to you, you work on it some more. It's a good programme, Fiona says, for people who are not focused.

Frances is a poet and a painter. When asked about goals, she surprised me by saying, "I like having goals" (she mentioned mastering her new computer and building a garden path). "I like projects." She likes lists too. (I know the feeling – tick something off. I've done something useful today.) And she likes to be challenged by goals that feel a bit beyond what she thinks she can achieve. "You find you can do it. It stretches you."

Ishy used not to set goals. "If you don't set goals, no one can hold you to account. I was not competitive, so what was the point?" Now, having just graduated from the School for Social Entrepreneurs, she is planning her own business, and does set goals, with a system to write them down and check on them. She still doesn't think she is goal-orientated, though – she just gets on with it. "My goal", she says, "is not to get to sixty and find that I didn't do it. Not to find that I had the opportunity to go white-water rafting and didn't do it." Although she has goals for the next couple of years, she says she is not good at middle-term goals. "Ten years ahead terrifies me. I'm terrified of my own mortality; death looming over me." With a father and two brothers who died young, perhaps that is not surprising. It has given her a huge zest for life. "You've got to love your life. I do, actually."

Lynn, with her husband Rob, has run a sandwich shop in central London for over twenty years. She spoke frankly: "I don't have time to have goals. I do what I have to do. We just muddle through." When they started, they thought the café would make a lot of money, but have long accepted that they just make ends meet. They'd like to retire in a couple of years, move to the country and have a dog, but as Lynn's pensionable age keeps going up (it is currently 63½), it seems an ever-receding possibility. So, plans, yes, but not goals.

Mark spoke passionately against goal-setting. "Beware of goals that can be reached," he said. "They're a mirage. Work for world peace if you like but don't expect to achieve it." When I asked him to elaborate, he wrote:

> If I set myself tough goals, I risk not achieving what I wanted, feeling that I'm a failure. So, logical person that I am, I set myself easier goals - that way, I'm assured easier success. If I fail at that easy stuff, of course, I'm a double failure. Bad idea, I feel ashamed. So I'll make the goals more attainable next time, lower the bar a little.
>
> I'm now embracing a shame-based way of life, based on the mantra: Help! Supposing I fail!
>
> It seems to me healthy to abandon goals and sink back into an acceptance that everything is part of a process. If I have to have targets, I'm better to make them the kind that one person can never reach and that don't massage my ego – world peace, the abolition of hunger. That way, I can spend my time putting one foot in front of the other, neither afraid of failure nor triumphant with success. Living, in other words.

A local builder, Michael, gave me a vivid example of the fallacy of goal-motivation, when he related the story of someone being dropped on to the top of Everest by a helicopter. "What's the point?" he asked. "It's the climbing that's the point; the journey to get there. Running a marathon", he said, "is about the running, not the getting there" – you could do that with no fuss on a bike or in a car.

Although we are bidden in the Gospels not to give too much thought for the morrow, some degree of planning is a necessary ingredient of everyday life. We need to grow or buy food to eat. But attaching too much importance to future goals may mean that we fail to have full awareness of the present. When we reach one goal, we might be so busy planning the next that we fail to take full pleasure in that present either. And goal posts have a habit of moving. Although goals presuppose outcomes,

outcomes do not always bear much relation to the original goal, either in failing to produce outcomes, or in producing outcomes of an unforeseen kind.

Goals are limiting. Career advisors' horizons are limited; how we develop is unpredictable: we often end up doing things we had never dreamt of, let alone planned. Some of the jobs I have done in my life I had never even heard of ten years before. If anyone had told me twenty years ago that I would have done some of the things I have done in the last fifteen, I would never have believed them.

If we set goals, they need to be flexible, to take into account the fact that we do not know what will happen. Every now and then we are reminded of the unpredictability of the universe. We have only to look at careful lives devastated by earthquake or civil war; at well-managed careers changed for ever by cancer or a car accident. The actor and director, Peter Capaldi, is quoted as saying, "I've never been able to make any plans. The only time I've tried to make plans the cosmic sledgehammer has intervened and something else has happened. You just have to wait and see what comes your way, so that's what I do" (*Independent*, 9 April 2011). Planning too often comes from assumptions about the future, from an expectation that we know what will happen, or even that we can control it. As Kathryn Schulz points out in her entertaining and thought-provoking, *Being Wrong*, from childhood on we seem predisposed to think that we *know*.

Taking out insurance policies is one acknowledgement of the uncertainties of life (although, interestingly "Acts of God" are generally excluded), but is financial recompense a complete and satisfying response? Allowing for the unexpected, indeed, in business parlance, "factoring it in", opening ourselves to its creative possibilities, will not only enrich the way we live our lives but contribute to a more fruitful outcome.

For me, creative growth is learning that there is much that I do not know, and to let go of my forward-looking compulsion:

needing to plan things, wanting to have *finished* things. In my writing, I have learnt *not* to sit at my computer for set hours every day, *not* to set myself a certain number of words to be written each week, allowing the Spirit room to breathe. I have recognised that I am more interested in dreams made concrete than achievable goals, and am trying to open up my life accordingly. Given my childhood behaviour, perhaps it is significant that I have twice put myself on a clowning course!

On the second occasion, which was quite recent and some twelve years after my first attempt, the emphasis of the course was not on failure but on connectedness. It was about giving a hundred per cent, about being emotionally transparent, and about spontaneity. There was to be no planning; we were asked to arrive fresh at every moment, paying attention to the inner core, and responding to whatever happened. The unexpected is a gift to accept and to be acted on with joy. It's a naked, vulnerable place to be, but profoundly fulfilling.

As the priest and clown, Roly Bain, has written:

The clown embodies and offers a world where different rules apply, a world that has been turned upside down and inside out, a playful world where the only rules are the law of love. (http://www.hospitalclown.com/)

Ultimately it's a world of healing, so perhaps it's not surprising that some of the most powerful expressions of clowning have been in refugee camps and children's hospitals.

* * *

This is not a philosophy of not looking where one is going; it is a philosophy of not making where one is going so much more important than where one is, that there will be no point in going. (Alan Watts, *The Way of Zen*. Penguin, 1970, p.145)

And what about luck? Whilst emphasising the need for preparation and application, people who talk about success sometimes mention their good fortune. We do not know what or whom we will meet that might change our lives, our expectations or our plans and how, if we meet them with all our attention and positive intent, our lives can be transformed. We might describe this process as "making our own luck".

Or we might consider the process as more significant. Mike is a former director of a London charity, and has spent most of his life in giving service to the community. His decision-making process, he has told me, is governed by his faith; guidance comes from synchronicity – a series of seeming coincidences, or glimpses of connection. What, I wondered, did he think about goals? Referring to the voluntary sector, he said,

> You do have to have goals. If you don't immerse yourself in the issue, live with it, the indication wouldn't have any energy around it. Having a goal – maybe a bit vague at the beginning – you try to achieve a change that you think is desirable. If you set about it and the energy doesn't increase and there's nothing to feed off, you move on to something else.

But how, I asked, did he tie in the concept of goals with living in the Spirit?

> The Spirit doesn't have goals; it has direction. You get an idea of what is called for from a combination of influences around you. I have to wait, sometimes months, for confirmation that what I'm thinking of is the right thing to do.

What we supply is the intention, and then we look for confirmation. Mike talked of a time when the information he needed arrived –

I hadn't even asked for it. This concern that I was holding seemed able to influence people I hadn't even spoken to. As creatures we have extraordinary capabilities we are barely aware of. Sometimes you can almost see the aura of energy in another.

You don't need to understand it, he says;

all you need to know is that you choose to interpret your experience and whether you can trust it. If there are several coincidences, and the idea doesn't leave you, you begin to believe you're on to something. It owns you. You must then ramp up your efforts and energies in that field. That's when you go for it. It's full on. You're done for!

In this sort of process, waiting seems inevitable, and waiting in an open kind of way, allowing possibilities to enter. Penny too has had this kind of experience. Having left behind her original career in the corporate sector, she worked for a while for a national charity before going abroad to do voluntary work. The charity she had been working for offered to keep her job open, but she declined. She didn't want the safety net of a job, in case what she did in India or Sri Lanka led to something.

Because the idea had come in [a Quaker] Meeting for Worship, I felt that trust all the time I was there. I was in the right place. I could trust my judgement of things. After my travels I lived on almost nothing, worked three days a week, was self-employed. I was waiting for "the thing", whatever it was going to be, marking time.

During this period Penny met someone she had studied with who was now working in the City, and was clearly successful in career terms. Penny's explanation of her life and her pleasure at her freedom – "I was proud of making that decision and coping well" – was met with a mixture of bewilderment and envy.

10

The matter in between

A man is a success if he gets up in the morning and goes to bed at night and in between does what he wants to do. (Bob Dylan)

I like to think of success as doing what you like but I've never really achieved it. (Neil)

What drives us? We have already seen that status, money and other material rewards play a large part in our push towards success, as does the need to do better than others, and cultural and parental expectations. One of the things that drive us, as we have also seen, is a fear of failure. Mark expressed this very powerfully when he said, "As someone growing up I felt it right and important to be a success, but only in order not to be a failure. I was very very very keen not to be a failure. I don't think I ever knew there was anything in between that was all right."

But is the drive also innate, part of our human identity? Is it part of our own wish to achieve, to express ourselves, to bring out what is within? Progress, the directional quality of our behaviour, the "and then and then" of our lives, is deeply ingrained. It seems to me that there are two parallel forms of human development. As babies we learn to move our heads, sit up, crawl, walk and talk, and take later steps at school. At the same time there develops a sense of who we are, our essential selves. Our parents encourage us as we move on from one stage of physical development to the next, sometimes in a rather competitive way, making comparisons about how quickly we take these steps with the progress of the children of their friends, or what is regarded as "normal". We need reassurance that our children are as special as we feel them to be.

But being special is more about who we are than about our tangible achievements. At what point does the "and then and then" stop? At what point, if ever, does the development of who we are take precedence over what we have done? With all this emphasis on "doing", do we consider the manner of our doing? Or how are we *being* when we are doing?

Judge not

Out beyond ideas of wrongdoing and rightdoing there is a field. I'll meet you there. (Rumi)

Most of us live with a running inner commentary of self-judgement, an expression of anxiety about not success but a wish not to fail. "Oh good, I made it. Will I manage the next stage? Did people think I was OK? Does my bum look big in this?" However much we try to curb it, our commentary extends to a critique of the behaviour, clothes, speech and looks of others. And we make comparisons. Whether the outcome of that comparison is a sense of personal success or failure will depend on the object of our comparison – someone higher or lower on the spectrum of our perception of success. Indeed, whether we tend to compare ourselves with people better or worse off than ourselves, more or less "successful", will generally depend on our general assessment of ourselves.

In any case, either form of comparison is dangerous. As Mike said when we discussed it, if you think you are a failure, "it stops you flourishing or doing what you could if you took the brakes off." If you think you are a success and you consider others to be a failure, he said, it is just as damaging to your spirit as the opposite. Quoting Jesus' comment that it is just as hard for a rich man to enter heaven as it is for a camel to pass through the eye of a needle, Mike emphasised the damage that arrogance and a sense of superiority can do. Judgement creates distance and blocks our compassion.

In his influential teaching about non-violent communication, Marshall Rosenberg offers an approach that refrains from making judgements. He suggests that the process has five different stages: (a) Observation of what does or doesn't contribute to well-being; (b) saying how you feel in relation to what you observe; (c) what you need or value in relation to what you observe; (d) clearly requesting that which would enrich your life without demanding and (e) saying the concrete actions you would like taken.

What is most arresting about his approach is that he regards not only criticism but praise and compliments as "life-alienating". "Compliments", he says, "are often judgments – however positive – of others. The beauty of appreciation is spoiled when people begin to notice the lurking intent to get something out of them" (185-6). In much the same way, Alfie Kohn distinguishes between different kinds of positive feedback: the problematic type, he feels, consists of "verbal rewards that feel controlling, make one dependent on someone else's approval" (2000: 96).

These challenging teachings have been a profound influence on Adam and Gillian in the way they bring up their daughter, Megan, now three years old. Like most parents, their starting point had been that without praise a child would not feel valued, but when Megan was born, they realised that babies don't have that kind of baggage; they come into the world expecting their needs to be met. In raising Megan, they want her to be affirmed for who she is rather than what she does; to be absolutely loved and accepted, without perpetual judgement, even of the positive kind. So they attempt not to praise her achievements. This is so contrary to our usual practice that it takes some getting used to. Indeed, Megan's grandmother says,

> I find it hard not to say "Hurrah" or similar when she first manages a somersault or sets the table but I can see what they

mean. I can see I was brought up with perpetual judgement and that this overemphasised a desire to succeed and gain approval. And this was reinforced by the similar style at school. We were even marked every week on our deportment and behaviour!

Gillian recognises that "all parents say that what they want is for their children to be happy", but feels that "most parenting does not prioritise the things that are most important". Adam said that their wish as parents is "to equip Megan as an adult to identify her needs, assert her needs, explain her needs and balance them against those of other people".

But no one lives in isolation, and other people's responses can be difficult. "We get a lot of stick," Adam said. Although they recognise that the behaviour of others – for instance, Adam's mother – comes from a real desire for the best for Megan, they find difficult and regard as manipulative comments such as "When you have eaten this rice cake, I will read to you." "The perception is that we have ceded discipline and control, that Megan rules the roost, and that that is deeply damaging for her and for us." That's not how they see it. "We allow her choices that are about her – when she goes for bed, for instance. We need to recognise the difference between her needs and her desires – and our own – and to be creative about what to do about the desires."

They recognise that schooling might be difficult. Gillian loved school, was competitive and good at it, and she can see that Megan might be just the same. "Fitting in is something she could do very easily, but I think it would damage her sense of worth as coming from within, and make her dependent on approval and disapproval". Or as Alfie Kohn would put it, become a "praise-junkie". They are thinking about sending Megan to a Steiner kindergarten, which, although structured in some ways, does not have tested objectives.

Having come across this way of raising children, they felt they had no choice. If it didn't feel so clear, Gillian said, they wouldn't be doing it. It's not easy. Without the usual judgemental tools, they find that they have to rely on being good role models themselves. When there is a way of being that they would like to affirm, they themselves have to model it, which they sometimes find quite demanding. Adam said that he knows that this way of bringing up a child is intrinsically right. But he also feels he has been influenced by seeing his own weaknesses, and where they come from, which is partly from his own upbringing. He is, he says, internally quite judgemental, a tendency reinforced by work.

They both feel strongly that this way has wider implications. As Gillian said,

If we want to create a better, peaceful world, we have to start with our parenting. How we parent can change the world. I don't want it to come across that we think we know it all, or that we're saying that everyone must do what we are doing. We don't. We are just doing what feels right for us now. Doing our best.

Adam is a civil servant but he finds that he is bringing even to this very conventional setting some of the same attitudes. When one of his staff did something well recently, he didn't say, "well done", which would have just brought a "thank you", but instead commented that the task had been done, and asked the staff member how he felt about it. The man opened up about how it had felt, and Adam not only received more information, but felt their exchange had contributed to building a relationship. He and Gillian both try to apply this way of non-judgemental being to work and in life. Gillian said how difficult it is for her now to receive even positive judgements – her inner response is: "I don't want that."

In Chapter 5 we considered acceptance as a response to

failure: our own and others'. Here, we are considering a more profound level of acceptance, in which we move away from making any kind of judgement at all. Instead of seeking affirmation from "being noticed, celebrated and praised", as Fr James said, "we need to be detached from these to find a place of real affirmation." Affirmation from within. Moving from judgement to acceptance, not sitting in judgement on ourselves or on others, is profoundly counter-cultural when every aspect of working life and sometimes our personal lives is subjected to assessment, weighing performance against expectation or others' achievements.

Process

"It's not the winning that matters, but the taking part" is a caricature of English sportsmanship that has often been used to excuse poor performance. As the BBC's cricket correspondent, Jonathan Agnew, recently said, "A good old defeat does not do anybody any harm." But maybe the old cliché represents a deeper understanding. The notion of success is to arrive at some pinnacle: a fixed, if temporary, state. That may be true of physical feats – the best that a body is capable of at any given time – but can never be true of our whole selves. There can be no end to the growth of our wisdom, our understanding, our love. Even as we age, and it seems as if our capabilities are shrinking, we can grow until the moment of our death – and who knows what we might grow into then.

In our exploration of the journey towards success, we have looked at goals, targets and outcomes but have missed out the vision, the content and the process. The incentive, our motivation, may come not from external factors, but from the attraction of what we are actually doing. We may enter into something simply because we want to, just feel like doing it, feel drawn to it, or because we like the challenge. It may be that in the process of doing it we find fulfilment. In those cases, the work, the action is likely to lead to a greater degree of satisfaction, indeed, to happiness.

Alfie Kohn's research has shown that success is more likely if our motivation is intrinsic.

> What does lead to excellence, then? This depends on what field and task we are talking about, but generally we find that people do terrific work when (1) they are inspired, challenged and excited by what they are doing, and (2) they receive social support and are able to exchange ideas and collaborate effectively with others (1993: 241).

Note the use of the phrase "terrific work". He is referring to work that is good in itself, not with reference to anything anyone else might be doing. And it is its own reward.

I recently watched a short film about a group of men freeing a hump-back whale that had got caught up in fishermen's nets, and was near to death. At first, one of the men swam near the whale, aware that the frightened animal could, with one blow, kill him. With his knife, first in the water, then with others in the boat, he slashed at the net, freeing first one dorsal fin, then the other, and finally the whole animal was free. As the whale swam off, the man turned to his companions, punched his fist in the air, and shouted: "We did it!" Success – and pure compassion.

It is possible to objectivise goals and outcomes; harder to do so for what lies in between: the actuality, the experience itself, in all its richness and complexity. To take another cliché, "Better to travel hopefully than to arrive": it's the journey, the process, that matters. If we do what we do from an authentic, centred position, surely that is all we are required to do or, more importantly, to be.

Ian described to me a part of his own recent journey. In November 2011, as protestors gathered to form an Occupy London group near the London Stock Exchange and outside St

Paul's Cathedral, Ian decided to visit them. He ended up staying for a month, sharing a tent, and in the clothes he stood up in. Finding a notion of success and achievement in that microcosm, he felt, was difficult. It was hard, he says, not to internalise the values of the dominant culture, hard not to think of himself as "doing something naughty". In any media debate, it seemed to be others who set the terms. Seeking a definition of success, Ian found himself falling back on his own basic principles; when they are supported by others, he says, "that *feels* like success".

Process, Ian says, is at the heart of the Occupy experience. There's dialogue, shared understanding, a feeling of people being listened to. The protestors are testing success, Ian says, in terms of the relationships they're building – with each other, and with other groups, such as the clergy at St Paul's. Concentrating on sharing what they believe brings unity amid an extraordinary diversity of backgrounds. Unlike his experience as a community worker, he says that at the encampment, everyone living in the same conditions means there is no distance, no status anxiety. Everything feels very natural; even normal economic transactions have disappeared. Occupy residents are living very much in a fluid present, allowing things to evolve. It is hard to imagine what the results of their actions will be and, unlike most of the society outside, that is not their preoccupation.

Focusing entirely on the result of our actions is to deny the richness of the experience. As Thomas Merton wrote:

> Do not depend on the hope of results. You may have to face the fact that your work will be apparently worthless and even achieve no result at all, if not perhaps results opposite to what you expect. As you get used to this idea, you start more and more to concentrate not on the results, but on the value, the rightness, the truth of the work itself. You gradually struggle less and less for an idea and more and more for specific people. In the end, it is the reality of personal relationship that

saves everything. ("A letter to a young activist")

The celebrated pianist, Arthur Rubenstein, had a more profound understanding of success than his own considerable musical achievements. "Of course there is no formula for success except perhaps an unconditional acceptance of life and what it brings."

Neale Donald Walshe considers not only that failure can be a positive, but that the whole concept is an illusion – one of what he calls the ten human illusions.

> Nothing you do is a failure but merely part of the process you have undergone to achieve what you are seeking to achieve, and to experience what you are seeking to experience…When you experience that which you are not, it is not a *failure* to experience but a way to experience That Which You Are…And so when what you call "failure" visits your life, embrace it lovingly…Put simply, the way to step outside of the illusion of Failure is simply to see everything as a part of your success…If you "succeed" at everything, then you will experience succeeding at nothing. You will simply feel you are doing what you are doing…*There is no such thing as failure.* There is only success, manifesting in its various aspects…*You never fail to succeed* (138-41).

But if failure is an illusion, isn't that automatically also true of success? In his poem, "If", Rudyard Kipling implies that both are dubious concepts. He not only urges us to treat triumph and defeat just the same, but calls them *"two impostors"*. What does that mean? In his introduction to a collection of Kipling poetry, Andrew Rutherford refers to "the impermanence, the transience – but not the worthlessness – of all achievement".

If they are impostors, what is our alternative focus? In the context of the poem, the poet seems to be referring to the unimportance of the end result. What counts are not the trappings of success and failure but the core of yourself. You strive to do the best you can. If what you do is considered as success or failure, it's just one of those things. Kipling's exhortation to treat triumph and defeat just the same does not shrink from an assessment but urges the reader not to allow either to affect his sense of self.

Creativity

When Frances talked of her art, she said that in both poetry and painting the success is the process itself.

> Before, you wonder if it will come off, and afterwards, you wonder if it has. Success is loving where you are. Writing or painting – it is so much more an exploration than an exposition. I slightly mistrust people who have got a lot to say. During the process of either, you think you know what you're doing – you can use words or paint. I'm very aware at the beginning that it's me doing it, but if there isn't a shift to not me doing it, but the thing being done, there isn't that kind of – [she fumbled for the right word] – explosion. It's what I do it for. That kind of recognition, like a relationship, that anything is possible.

The common feeling of being painted, written, through was expressed by another poet: "Someone else wrote this. It has arrived from I know not where. There it is and I'm amazed."

The creative process has its own momentum. It is unusual for a finished product – a book or a painting – to end up exactly as planned. In the writing of a novel the characters can take over. And allowing that to happen can have a profound effect on the maker.

> Only art as meditation allows one to let go of art as production à la capitalism and return to art as process, which is the

spiritual experience that creativity is about. Only art as meditation reminds people so that they will never forget that the most beautiful thing a potter produces is... the potter (Fox, 192).

Creativity is not confined to creating works of art. The term describes an approach to the whole of life, allowing playfulness and spontaneity to enter our lives; accepting some slack; letting go of the need to control and direct every move. Creativity is living adventurously. Imagine leaving the day open, with nothing in the diary or on the to-do list, allowing things to emerge as they will. Wander outside and see whom you meet, what you find, what you are moved to explore. Such formlessness feels risky: there is a fear that nothing will happen – indeed – or maybe something unexpected will greet our consciousness. Can we cope with the unexpected? Can we make ourselves vulnerable to the unknown? At the very least, a more fallow day will allow creative thoughts to germinate and at some future time to jump into consciousness.

In our society, the general approach is a busy one. We fill up our days; assess others by what they achieve, and congratulate ourselves on how much we do. It is all too easy to con ourselves with the empty shell of practice or busy ourselves with a false sense of achievement when actually we are just creating a façade of busyness. But it is not only busyness that is the problem but the mechanistic way in which we live much of our lives. Routine, repetition, conditioned behaviour – these are stifling to the imaginative spirit. When we open ourselves up to spontaneity, we enable creativity to enter our lives.

But when we play, truly play like a kid does, it is the process that becomes the point. Can we allow ourselves to make it up as we go along, see where our imagination takes us, and forget to self-edit so much? That would mean being OK with an outcome that others might dislike. (Elizabeth Evitts Dickinson on http://observatory.designobserver.com)

Success and failure are only recognised with hindsight: we don't know what they are until after the event. In the doing we are rarely conscious of any such concept. In development work, for instance, any notion of failure or success is external. On the ground, in the moment, no such notion arises. What is going on is about a relationship, a connection, maybe a small shift in understanding or attitude. It is clear when it happens, and it may be far-reaching in the life of the individual concerned, but it is not measurable in any terms that would make sense from the outside.

In our personal lives, too, entering into the fullness of the moment demands complete and intentional attention. It may be that in the process of sitting an examination, taking a test or competing with others, the notion of winning, of success, crosses our thoughts, but the moment such self-consciousness interrupts our concentration, the performance is likely to falter. As Tennessee Williams said, "Success is shy – it won't come out while you're watching." Only when we are immersed in the process of what we are doing, will there be an opportunity for creative take-off, for us to feel inspired, to do something beyond our usual capabilities.

The opportunity to lose ourselves in what we are doing comes only if we are engaged in something that enlivens us. Albert Schweitzer considered that "success is not the key to happiness. Happiness is the key to success. If you love what you are doing, you will be successful." That has certainly been my experience. I have been fortunate in my life to be involved in work that has been important to me. When I first managed the careers of writers as an independent literary agent, I decided that I would represent only the work that I loved. Feeling that this was self-indulgent and unlikely to make my living, I thought I had better take on a couple of part-time activities to pay the bills. The extra activities did not work; the agency boomed. I was doing what I loved; was persuasive in my own love of the work, and others were convinced.

When women are considering starting a microbusiness, they are often driven by external circumstances: the lack of alternatives, the need to make money, the views of others. It's important to encourage them to think of what matters to them: "Don't do something just because you think it will make money. Remember that you have to spend something like eight hours a day doing this. Do something you really want to do. Think of your dreams." When they listen to their own intuition, the success of their ventures is often astonishingly swift.

But, as one friend I spoke to pointed out, in the practical everyday world, you need outcomes. "I care about the outcome of a builder finishing the job," she said, "and he cares about it, so he can get paid." If someone is paid for a service, the outcome of their work is important; their livelihood depends on producing what was expected, on pleasing the client. Reputation matters, although it is as much about honesty, reliability and good work as about a particular outcome. She also mentioned the cooking of a meal. The process is enjoyable, but it would be pointless if there was no outcome of a meal to eat.

Process must not be ignored, but achievement still matters. Our gifts are there to be expressed, even if there is no need for them to acquire the gloss of public congratulation.

The truth of the maxim "the medium is the message" has very broad applications. Just as in great art, form and content have a symbiotic relationship, so in the wider world, too, process and outcome are mutually defined. Gardening is a perfect example of the interconnection. To grow anything takes time, and requires some vision of what the future will hold. Guarding against pests and disease, birds and inclement weather may interfere with our best endeavours. The plants may simply fail to grow. Uncertainty is part of the package. But the activity is for many the main pleasure; the feel of the soil, being in the open air, the physical exercise, the handling of the seeds and plants; delight at the appearance of a tender shoot; involvement in the cycle of seasons. The picking and eating of the fruit and vegetables is part of a continuum of contentment. Of course, for farmers it is a business, and livelihoods hang on it; and, for some, competitiveness – about the biggest marrow, tomato or potato – can once again creep in.

The South African Eden Grace, writing about the Quaker decision-making process, says:

> We value process over product, action or outcome. The *process* of reaching a decision yields more *results* than the decisions themselves. Attention to the Divine movement in the community is, in fact, the source of decision and action, so that process and outcome are ideally two sides of the same sacramental experience ("An introduction to Quaker Business Practice").

Helen spent ten years teaching in Taiwan. In such a collectivistic society, she said, process matters. She told me a story of a paintball event that some young people organised. Very few people turned up, apparently, but it was regarded as a success. What mattered was not just the game but the whole process: meeting friends, bonding, having a meal together.

Exit strategy

In 2010 two programmes that I had been instrumental in starting celebrated their tenth anniversaries. One was a mobile library for homeless people in London. It is regarded as successful: it is appreciated by its users, it is well used, the number of centres it serves has increased, it has been replicated in different parts of Britain and abroad, and each year it wins prizes. But true success would be if it had done away with the need for its services; if access to public libraries did not depend on having an address, so that there was no further need for a specialist service. There is some hope: some libraries are actively looking at ways of being more inclusive in their services.

The other was a microcredit programme in the East End of London, enabling women from many different cultures to start their own businesses. Although it too has won prizes, and a party was held for the anniversary when beneficiaries stood to speak of the difference it had made to their lives, the party also marked the closure of the programme. It was no longer fulfilling the purpose for which it had been set up. Success or failure?

A friend of mine, visiting a programme for Pakistani women in North London that she set up some years ago, was thrilled to see it up and running. The women hailed her as the instigator of its success, but the true success is that she is no longer needed. As many involved in charitable programmes know, the fulfilment of an exit strategy is their ultimate success.

11

Transformation II: some different stories

In writing this book, I have come across a number of people who have left well-paid or high-profile careers – in theatrical production, merchant banking or the senior ranks of the civil service – to go into the voluntary sector or to fulfil a long-cherished dream. Such people have been content to leave behind the trappings of success for something which for them is more meaningful.

An extreme example is Barbara, who for three years lived in the presidential suite of a five star hotel, and left it to sleep on the floor of a rented room. For six months her furniture, clothes and books – all her possessions – were held on to by the customs authorities, because she refused to pay them a bribe. She lived in borrowed clothing until finally the US Embassy sorted it out. "Most of my life has been either at the top or at the bottom...all part of the adventure of life..."

Barbara feels the need for the freedom to redefine success. At the age of five, she says, she knew she wanted to help poor people. Feeling that it didn't matter what she did to begin with, Barbara went into banking. She says of that time,

I already had a sense of the distortions in the modern day use of money from its origins in barter. I could see the potential for the financial crises that have happened. I needed to do things that were real, not virtual. When we came off the gold standard there was no equivalence. Governments all over the world have been printing money.

Barbara's main considerations in every move since have been: "Is

it something that's needed?" and "If I don't do it, who will?"
"The potential impact of my work is much more important to me
than the status, income or job title that it gives me."

The big decision came when, after a long career in banking,
she was asked by the US government to start a very large, high-
profile poverty alleviation initiative in a field she knew nothing
about in a totally foreign country, culture and language. The
challenge of starting a new initiative all on her own, without
even family support near by, was huge. "I was so scared. What
would happen if I couldn't do it? I didn't know anything."

That Christmas, she walked along the beach in Maine to
weigh up her decision.

Do I stay in a comfy job, and make everyone happy, except
myself, knowing I am not helping anyone out of poverty? I
fast-forwarded to the last day of my life. Staying would be
doing something that would make people think I was
successful. But what would I think of myself on my deathbed?
Rubbish.

Or do I take this opportunity, and risk my whole career?
Risk the possibility of being a public failure after losing all the
starting capital and failing the people it was meant for...

Barbara decided to take the risk, and says she feels proud of this
decision. Though she might fail, in the best case she might
achieve something really big, so the personal sacrifice had to be
worthwhile. After five years building the programme, she went
on to found another similar one, before joining one of the biggest
organisations in the sector and gaining some very valuable
experience in the politics of the non-profit industry. After fifteen
years in banking and a further fifteen working on poverty alleviation programmes, it was now time, she said, to embark on her
third career.

Since we spoke in 2010, she has started a new job which will bring together all the threads of her life's work. It seems that that decision made on a beach in Maine all those years ago did indeed change her life.

* * *

Penny has a degree in psychology and philosophy, and started her career in the corporate sector. She wanted to work for one of the biggest companies in the field of psychometrics, and in order to do so needed a Master's in occupational psychology. While working for this qualification, Penny had a moment of clarity: a realisation that she was not going to be able to work in the corporate sector – and she wondered what she was going to do with her Master's.

Eventually, she decided to follow her original plan for the time being, and found that she was learning a good deal from working in Human Resources, finding a motivation questionnaire particularly interesting, especially

the various factors that can be motivating (such as money, praise or control over your work) and how some of these can also be de-motivators. So, hardly anyone is de-motivated by being paid more money, but some people are de-motivated by being given too much control because they like to have more guidance.

After two years, Penny left to go to Friends of the Earth. One of her colleagues said, "I can't believe you're leaving. I thought you were on your way to becoming MD."

After a time abroad, she waited for clarity about what her path was to be. "Contentedness is an attitude of mind towards where you are right now, so the waiting wasn't hard, because I had the trust. Something I've held on to – making conscious choices, and therefore being content with where you find yourself."

Eventually Penny came across "The Reader Organisation", based in Liverpool, and felt she had found what she had been looking for. Their key programme, "Get into Reading", brings people together through weekly read aloud groups, where people can choose to read and are invited to give personal responses. The groups, led by volunteers and trained project workers, meet in a variety of locations – libraries, care homes, prisons and hospitals. Penny was passionate about the programme and determined to bring it to London. Without pay, she worked hard to get the necessary funding and in 2009 obtained three years' funding, including her own salary. She is now one of five staff in London, and they are recruiting for more.

Although she comes from a high-achieving family, her parents are fine with her change in direction. Her father's appreciation of his luck in doing something he really enjoys has been very influential. Penny said, "I don't really think about success and failure. The world's view of success is something I've been moving away from."

Penny is now in her early thirties, and has recently considered moving within her organisation to be closer to her family. It would mean doing the work that she is currently co-ordinating in her area. When she was asked, "How would you feel about not being in charge of things?", her response was, "'Well, you can't know me very well to ask that.' I don't mind as long as I enjoy what I'm doing, and am making a contribution. It's a balance of being where your heart is and living up to your potential of what you could be doing."

* * *

For ten years June was an independent literary agent. She represented one of the biggest US publishers, built up her own client base, was tough, driven, and highly regarded. She doesn't remember being ambitious or intending to go into publishing.

After "failing" to get into Oxbridge, finding university disappointing and several false starts afterwards, she found herself saying to her uncle: "I'm going into publishing," and it became true. June then spent about six years in a prestigious publishing house, mainly, as she put it, as a minion, until she had had enough of not having "a proper job". Eventually she became managing editor of another house and was given her head. It was a good time until her boss, previously supportive, found her and her success difficult. At that point she felt she had had enough, and said to herself, "I can't work for other people, I've got to work for myself."

June went to New York and agreed with a big US company to represent their books in the UK. The move to become an agent was not, she said, to make money. "It was about independence and doing things the way I wanted to do them, and not having some rotten person at my elbow telling me I'd done something wrong." She started her agency in a recession – as she said, if you can survive in a recession, you can survive anything. After her first trip to New York, her husband decided to go back to law school, and she became the breadwinner. She began to build up her own client list and was, she said, "quite good at selling because I knew about buying as an editor".

June had never wanted to have children but in her late thirties something happened to change her mind. In a workshop exercise at a summer school she attended, participants were paired up, and after chatting were asked to introduce each other to the group. June told her partner: "I'm not going to have children." He introduced her by saying, presumably by mistake, "June is going to have children." She was upset and furious, and it was only in talking to a counsellor friend that she began to understand that unconsciously she did want to have children.

Looking back, she realises that she thought that if she wanted to have children she would. She was used to things working out by then; she was used to success. After trying for about a year, she had to have an operation to remove all the fibroids and then became pregnant. She continued rushing around, first to New York, then to the Frankfurt Book Fair, and then she discovered that the baby had died in the womb. She gave birth to Philip stillborn. No one, she said, had told her that she should rest. Or that the pregnancy might fail if she didn't.

At that point, June took a sabbatical from the agency to give her time to look at the "failure", and never returned. The decision to sell up, she says, was not just a grief reaction; when she got pregnant she had already decided that she wanted to move on, and this confirmed it. Nor was it just the death itself that served as a transformative turning point in June's life: it was the response from other people. Having generally considered publishers as "the opposition, if not the enemy", she was astonished when some two hundred of them wrote to her when Philip died. As she wrote:

> nothing could make your heart beat again or put the leaves
> back on the November branches or, with the turn of the
>   month,
> make the hanging of Christmas holly bearable.
>
> Like sweets in wartime, though, I hoarded
> scores of unexpected letters, rationing myself to one a day.
> I never knew I had so many weeks of friendship.
> (From the title poem in *Bowing to Winter* by June Hall.
> Bath: Belgrave Press, 2010)

This outpouring of compassion changed her view of human nature. By then, she told me, the concept of success "was less important, and the concept of human nature being more good and generous became much more so".

On leaving the agency, June trained for four years in counselling and began to write poetry seriously. She had to do, as she put it, "a lot of unlearning". A year to the day of Philip's death, June discovered she was pregnant again, and went on to have two more children, born when she was 41 and 43. She said of parenting: "There's no way I was going to be a successful parent. I had no idea it was going to be such a manual job. I did work hard at it, reading books and going to groups. It was very hard for me. I was too old, too tired, had too many changes – career, house and having children all at the same time." She confessed, "I've always had a tendency to bite off big bites and find them impossible to chew."

But life's challenges had not finished with June. In the late 1990s she was diagnosed with Parkinson's disease, and a few years later her husband developed cancer of the oesophagus. Seven years on, they are both still here, and the children are moving towards independence. June is glad now that she was successful as an agent. Having seen her mother struggle with poverty, she knows that without the financial rewards life would have been a lot harder.

She deliberately keeps her counselling practice small, and treats writing poetry as a job too – it's good to have the two kinds of work in her life. After nearly twenty years as a counsellor, she no longer feels a fraud or an impostor because, she says, it's coming from an authentic place.

At the end of our afternoon together, I asked June if life was good. "Yes," she replied without hesitation, "it is – I feel very lucky."

* * *

My own career path was somewhat similar to June's, and indeed it was from her I learnt my trade. When I sold my own agency after fourteen years (for very different reasons than those that motivated June), I was led to move into another world. I started a community centre in the East End of London and worked as a volunteer with street homeless people. Subsequently I set up microcredit programmes, became a research associate for the Prison Reform Trust, and a facilitator for a conflict resolution programme. And I now write books.

The contrast between my previous world and the one I live in now was highlighted a few years ago when I walked down a street in the West End of London, and passed a smart bar, outside which were sitting two publishers with whom I had done much business in the past. I was tramping purposefully along the road, dressed in a fleece, flat shoes with a knapsack on my back. The two editors – both people I like and respect – were sitting in casual elegance, each with a glass of white wine in hand. We greeted each other warmly, they asked politely about what I was doing, and about my next book, but the contrast between the sort of books I write, and the mega-sellers that engage their attention was obvious to us all. They were kind but really not at all inter-ested. In leaving the profession I had gone off the radar. Fortunately, I am a realist and would not have expected anything else – and it made me chuckle.

The Open Wing Trust has recently been set up to give support and small grants to those who take a financial risk in moving into work with and for those in need.

12

"Re-imagine Success"

Life is too important to be wasted in yearning to be rich, famous, good looking, popular, or pretty, or in dreading being poor, unknown, ignored, or ugly. These things become unimportant, as though they were pebbles alongside a dazzling diamond. You – your true self – have always been and will always be a diamond. (Anthony de Mello, quoted in Townsend, 71)

If A is success in life, then A = x+ y + z. Work is x, play is y and z is keeping your mouth shut. (Albert Einstein, in conversation with Samuel J Woolf, Berlin, Summer 1929)

As we saw in Chapter 1, Western society is submerged in a culture of success and celebrity. Although there has been no change in the adulation of fame and glamour, the gloss of visible wealth and property has been distinctly tarnished by the banking collapse and the UK MPs' expenses scandal. We have seen – and found distasteful – the lengths to which our representatives will go to acquire more than others, more than is fair. The looting during the riots of 2011 also showed the lengths to which people will go to acquire what is valued in society. Suddenly, wealth as a marker of success is a little more questionable.

In the first two chapters we looked at an objective and measurable concept of success, and how others see us. We have considered goals and process, and failure in both its negative and surprisingly positive aspects. So, how else might we envisage success? In this chapter we consider more subjective definitions: success viewed from within, as a state of mind, in relationship, and as a more lasting way of life.

There comes a time in some people's lives when the whole success culture ceases to have meaning. After half a lifetime of unquestioningly climbing the ladder, first of academic and then career progression in the civil service, Susan decided to leave her job. It was partly in recognition that she did not want her whole life to have been with one employer, and partly that she and her husband had decided to do something together. When her husband died suddenly, she kept to her original decision to leave the civil service. Subsequently, she remembers going for job interviews with the same old attitude, determined to succeed, to pass the interview, whether or not the job was right for her. But eventually she found another way of life. For the past eleven years, Susan has worked in the charitable sector, as an employee, a trustee, and in a voluntary capacity. Since that time of major life change, she says her attitude has also changed. She no longer has two lives with wardrobes to match: she is one person, herself, motivated by what impassions her, what will make a difference. She tries to live her testimony to integrity, trying not to fly, going on her bike to meetings with City types, regardless of what they think.

Beyond success

In most arenas of life we know that correctness and efficiency are not all. What someone brings to their work, for instance, is their whole self, how they interact with others, characteristics such as generosity and humour. In education it is not the rightness or wrongness of the answer but the sight of an original mind at work that lifts a piece of work beyond the ordinary.

In musical performance, even when a note is reached, sung or played in tune, plain correctness is not the point. Beauty, creative interpretation, depends on an ineffable something that is brought to it. Perfection is a static concept whereas remarkable art of any kind engages with a Spirit that is dynamic. The creative process goes beyond the individual, who often feels she is being played, written, painted through. Trish is an actor. She feels strongly that her audience must get what they came for. "I need to make it as good as I can for them. I don't think it has anything to do with me personally." She agreed that in any work of art, there is a sense of being an instrument of interpretation. "As an actor you get rid of yourself anyway. You're a character."

Geoffrey also spoke of the limitations of the concept of success: "When something is an act of exploration, growing organically, it's harder to talk about success or failure. That's true of a lot of things we do, such as performing a Beethoven string trio or mentoring a difficult child. Even if I were note-perfect, that would make me aware there's more to do."

Theatre director and workshop leader, Richard Olivier, exhorts us to "re-imagine" success in a way that takes fear of failure out of the equation (www.oliviermythodrama.com). We need, he says, to move away from "current definitions of success" which "are all too often limited to money and fame, supported by the apparently insatiable desire of the global capitalist mindset and the self-inflating vanity of a media obsessed with superficial appearance". Using Shakespearean cosmology, he suggests ways in which to look at the roles we play in the world. A more helpful definition of success, he suggests, would be the balance of four engagements, with:

1 the other, which leads to the ability to engage with
2 the self
3 work
4 the more than human world.

If we pay insufficient attention to any of these four, we will feel an unease that needs to be addressed.

"The tragedy of our time", says Olivier, "is that it doesn't value plurality of roles, only the one through which we add financial value." It is easy for us to get stuck in this role, living in a world in which answers to "what do you do" define us. As we have seen, the general view of success is wedded to this directional role, a role in which material outcomes are the only markers of worth. Specialisation in our work leads to a narrowing of our place in the world; climbing up the ladder, we can find, as they say, that it is leaning against the wrong wall.

I find the concept of balance between these four areas of engagement helpful. I am interested, though, in the order in which Richard Olivier has put the first two. Is it not possible to have an engagement with self without the aid of another? Hubert, for instance, says that part of his life journey is to facilitate for himself what that engagement with the other can bring. I too have trodden that path. In the wake of the break-up of a long-term relationship in 2003, I went walkabout, spending some months in remote parts of the UK, trying to make the move, as Henri Nouwen has put it, from loneliness to solitude. In fact, it is only, I believe, from a place of healed wholeness that engagement with the other will be truly authentic.

When people talked about what really mattered in their lives, it was generally of relationships that they spoke. Indeed, although many said that their greatest success was in the field of relationship, I had a feeling that their use of the term "success" was an attempt to fit their response into what they assumed I needed from them. When I mentioned to Geoffrey that in our discussions he had talked almost exclusively of work, he said it might stem from his unease with the use of the term "success" in inappropriate ways. "It's not", he said, "the way I like to think about relationships."

In fact, I echo his discomfort. How can we apply the word "success" to how we relate to one another? It's as if we were setting up the attainment of some measurable relationship goal, a yardstick by which to measure it. Is the quality of our relationship to be measured by others' expectation, or our own?

Is there a scale, or some sort of competition – can there be more or less success than others? My marriage ended in divorce, as many do. Yet at no time have I thought of it as a "failed marriage". What an abrupt and negative term to encompass all the hours and days, the love and laughter, home- and child-making in the decades of living together.

Mark had no such qualms: "The biggest failure of my life was the marriage. It must be a failure by definition. The 'I do's' are to make it work. And it didn't work." When he left his wife in 2002, he wasn't sure he had done the right thing, but is absolutely sure now that he did. "It would have been more miserable if I'd stayed." Then, thinking about it, he conceded, "But it didn't feel like a failure. I felt hurt beyond measure."

If we cannot sum up a marriage in such an absolute and objective way, the same must apply even more strongly to life in general. A successful life? How can we sum up the complexities, the infinite richness, of any life? In any case, what do we know even of our own life, let alone that of another? Who are we to judge? What does "making it" mean? How can such a judgement have an objective reality? Any act will bear the unique quality of the person or people performing it. Achievement will be in a particular way, of a particular kind. The different strengths and weaknesses will be reflected in the process and in the end result. With the distance of hindsight or the view of an outsider, it may appear to have an objective quality, but that is only part of the story.

At a turning point in her life, when a huge decision had to be made, Barbara says that she "fast-forwarded" to the last day of her life. She looked at her options, and considered how others would view her, and how she would view herself – and it was her sense of self that won through. In the end, she said, it came down to "the purpose for which we were born. *Tikkun olam*" (Hebrew for "healing the world").

What do we leave behind? Andy brought up the question of

legacy:

> How will I know if I have been successful? It has to be about people, not material objects. If you've made your mark, however small, in making the world a better place for others. If you have left behind a trail of broken hearts, dysfunctional families or broken employees, it's not a success. As we age, we all become the same. Material objects have no value. And then he quoted a favourite Quaker piece of advice: "Attend to what love requires of you."

Other comments included:

> The underlying script of my life is: Let's each of us do what we are called to do, have some aptitude for and feel comfortable with, and it might come out in the end. I'm motivated much more by that.

> Now I'm young and can be selfish. I have passion about work and my interests, a pony at home. But later, I'd like a combination of work I enjoy and a happy family life. Emotional wellbeing is what makes a successful life. Nice friends. It's a waste of a life to do something you don't enjoy. I wouldn't want either work or family to get in the way of the other.

Even in the inner landscape of success, lifestyle gurus have created a ladder to climb, applying the same external concepts of goals and outcomes as in our outer lives. But there other ways of dealing with inner discernment. If success is happiness, relationship, a way of being, then it acquires quite a different profile. Steady, continuing contentment. To have contentment in life, we need to let go of any striving for success. To let go of the need to have control over our lives. To let go, full stop. In letting go, allowing life to evolve, listening to our inner self and acting in truthful response, all that is needful will be shown.

Robert Holden, the creator of a coaching programme called Success Intelligence, outlines a plan for living "a truly rich life that creates more soulful success for yourself and those around you". "Success", he says, "is more than a 'to do list', a business card or a frantic race – it is about soul, love, authenticity and following your joy." The impressive sound-bites on their website include:

Success is not driving yourself harder, it is about letting go of what blocks your heart.

A successful life can only ever be the one you are living now.

If your definition of success has little or no measure of love in it, get another definition.

Many of the people I spoke to echoed this emphasis on inner values and self-affirmation. Seventeen-year-old Raymond felt that success was "being happy and having money to, like, not be a stress. Family, stable job so I don't worry. The more you worry, the more you waste life. Success is knowing you've done well, and tried your hardest, even if you fail." Rob agrees with Bob Dylan – success is about doing what you want: in his case, a bit of birdwatching. "Not quite sure what I mean by this, but it's to make your inner self happy." Ishy felt that success was very subjective and that it was more about how you see yourself than about how others see you. "If you grow as a person, you will rate yourself by your own standards." Other comments included: "To me success is happiness for the greatest period of time"; "being the best person you can be".

For many people, too, it is about contributing, service, giving back to society: "Success is when you have made a positive difference to someone's life." And the difference can be made by very little – a smile in the street, picking up a child's rattle on a bus. At the time of writing, an artist is running a campaign on London Underground to collect stories of "random acts of kindness" (art.tfl.gov.uk/actsofkindness). In measuring success, it is all too easy to be swayed by materialistic yardsticks – size, quantity, time-frame. But we underestimate the importance, and the frequency, of small deeds of love, the large amount of generosity that people give to each other all the time. In an act of generosity, a holistic approach is needed both for the giver and the receiver. In acting from a wholeness of being towards the wholeness of someone else, the act itself becomes reciprocal. Transformation is in the relationship, the love. Giving someone a bed for the night is a response from the heart. Such an act may take place in many circumstances, but it is one of generosity, solidarity, stemming from an individual relationship.

Susan has come to feel that successful people are those "who do something to change the world; have a vision, live it and make it a reality." She feels that the Joseph Rowntree Charitable Trust, of which she is a trustee, funds people like that, and she gave as an example Clive Stafford Smith, who represents people on Death Row, and is working to close Guantanamo Bay. "Success is building the Kingdom of Heaven. All right, we won't achieve it, but there are milestones along the way."

Margaret felt that "it's how you conduct yourself, your perception of how you're handling your life. Success is humility and compassion. Inner reverence and the acceptance that you could be wrong. If you are, it's not failure but an opportunity to get it right." Margaret has spent some forty-five years in teaching, both children and adults, mainstream and special needs, in the UK, and latterly in India. Asked how her views applied to education, she said, "You value the time you spend with the children, and they with you. You hope that they will use knowledge constructively in whatever field they choose. If you're not striving too hard for personal success, you can use that to elicit a sense of achievement in others."

* * *

We looked earlier at the short-lived nature of success. What we are talking about here is something more lasting. As Guy Finley says in his book, *The Secret of Letting Go*, "the real successes in life are more an awakening than they are an arrival at a thrilling but temporary destination" (Llewellyn Publications, 2011, pp. 229-30).

In this new view of success, the rewards are many and various. Most of all, a sense of self-belief will contribute to a more positive contribution to the world.

> Believing that this time we will succeed where in the past we have failed, or failed to try; believing the best of ourselves even when we are intimately familiar with the worst and the merely average; believing that everything in us that is well-intentioned will triumph over all that is lazy or fickle or indifferent or unkind: this is wrongness as optimism – an endlessly renewable over-extended faith in our own potential. (Schulz, 338)

Passing on the baton

Part of our re-imagining success is realising that what we wish for the next generation has little to do with wealth and status. When I asked John what success meant to him, he talked with pride of his son, who is a gardener, and also works as a carer for his wife. When I asked what that had to do with success or failure, John said, "He's a total success, just an unusual one, as a human being." There was an underlying and unspoken assumption that others might think his son a failure because he doesn't have a "good" job.

Many others mentioned their children. The success – or self-fulfilment – of Mark's children matters to him. He wants them to have the perspective and the material means to achieve what they want to do. He says he honestly doesn't mind what that is. "The best I can do as their father is to give them the opportunity and sometimes the money to follow their nose." Alex's life so far has been complicated. He has twice been married to women of different cultures. When living in Malaysia, he worked on low pay as a microbiologist and supported his wife's career by looking after the children. Back in the UK after the divorce, he was unable to get a job in his field after his period abroad, and worked for many years as a chauffeur. He struggled for a long time to get his children over to the UK, and to have some influence in their lives:

> I wanted to work things out for the kids. I always knew things would turn out: they generally do. Some cycles work out earlier than others – may not happen in the conventional order. The children have been more important than my career. Now they're sorted I'm much happier, and I can concentrate on the next step.

Now in his forties, Alex is qualifying as a teacher and feels very optimistic about the future. His wishes for his own children are that they are happy, reach the goals they set themselves, and are at peace with themselves.

Susan does not have children, but in the latter part of her career, her focus turned towards mentoring and helping the next generation to do well. Like children, she wanted them to be happy, to surprise themselves by achieving more than they expected they could.

I too feel I am stepping back. In the last couple of years, I have had the privilege of finding someone else to work with. Isebail (Ishy) ran Street Cred, the microcredit programme in the East End of London, and was keen to get overseas experience. We went together to Ghana to set up a programme, which the women named *Yen Daakye* ("our future"); she did the follow-up trip, and after our joint trip to start the scheme in another region, she has taken over the whole programme. Ishy is now setting up a social enterprise to initiate and support microcredit programmes both in the UK and abroad. I feel I have handed on the baton.

The significance of a life is generally judged after the life has been lived, by acknowledgement in an obituary or, ultimately, by history. Many people, hugely successful in their field in their own lifetimes, are now forgotten. The greatness of others, unrecognised in their lifetimes, sometimes comes to light decades or even centuries later. Their legacy, life after death, has been lasting. Would they be classed as successful? Probably not. Important, influential, great, perhaps, but not successful. Success, it seems, is quickly come and gone, and is not necessarily a testament to greatness.

A fine line

So, what makes the difference between success and failure? As we have seen, they are closer to each other than we think. Many things are both, or can be perceived as either. In many cases, trying to make a judgement is pointless; imposing that kind of viewpoint is irrelevant. What is important is how the situation is in all its positive and negative aspects, with all the subtleties of its impact.

David Hillson uses the Taijitu symbol of yin yang to demonstrate his vision of success and failure.

He suggests that

instead of being seen as a duality perhaps they should be seen as two sides of a single unitary phenomenon, that we would do well to keep both aspects in view and to maintain a balanced perspective. If white in the Taijitu symbol represents success, and black is failure, then we see success gradually increasing to a point where it leads to failure... However we also see that failure increases until it leads to success... It is also, however, usually true that when success flourishes most strongly it contains the seed of failure, and when we are at the deepest and darkest point of failure then a glimmer of success may be detected

with "a repeating pattern of mutual synergies between positive and negative" (Hillson, 17, 142).

Let us return to Kipling and his challenging pair of lines:

If you can meet with Triumph and Disaster
And treat those two impostors just the same...

What a high degree of detachment is called for to treat triumph and defeat, success and failure, just the same. Can we really rise above the exhilaration of the one and the pain of the other? Detach ourselves from ambition and the fruits of our labour? Recognise that seemingly different outcomes are interconnected, that in the long term all is one? It's a life-time's journey. But even if we can imagine that journey, if we also believe that success and failure are impostors, what do we put in their place? It is generally accepted that success is "good", failure "bad". But a crucial, and largely unrecognised, fact about success and failure is that they are *morally neutral*. One can succeed at something which makes a positive or negative impact on the world. Killing a man or growing a flower. It is the content and the context of the act which determine its moral quality.

That means that we must look elsewhere for what is truly important. Why are we trying to be successful? What *for*? What are we trying to be successful *at*?

What has come out of conversation with many people of all ages is that what they most value – what they feel will matter as they lie on their death beds – is to have lived an authentic life, to have fulfilled their potential and used their gifts, and to have made a difference, to have lived a compassionate life. Relationship matters.

If I look back on various periods of my life, I don't see them in terms of success and failure. I did what felt right at the time, however differently I might do it now. I don't, on the whole, have regrets, except about being unkind or ungenerous. Hindsight, it seems to me, is an unhelpful perspective. It was as it was. It now is as it is. And will be as it will be. We just have to get on with it, being open and alive to the possibilities that are offered. We are who we are with all our gifts and fallibility, our vulnerability and our potential for greatness. We do not need the masks we hide behind, the roles we inhabit, to compensate for feelings of unworthiness. We do not need to project our own fear of failure or success on to celebrities. If there is such a thing as being a failure it is, perhaps, not to fulfil our potential, to realise our gifts, to be who were meant to be. This failure may take the form of an unwillingness to try, or a use of our talents for selfish and unjust ends. This is true of ourselves as individuals, as communities, and collectively as a species.

Rob who, with his wife, has run a sandwich shop for the last twenty years, pondered the subject. "Success and failure? Do you think there's much difference?"

"What do you think?"

"Not much. A fine line, I would say."

13

Another dimension

Be in Truth eternal, beyond earthly opposites. Beyond gains and possessions, possess thine own soul. (Bhagavad Gita, 2:45)

He is glad with whatever God gives him, and he has risen beyond the two contraries here below; he is without jealousy, and in success and failure he is one. (ibid, 4.22)

At the core of the Alternatives to Violence Project is a mandala expressing the fundamental philosophy of this conflict resolution programme. At the heart of the mandala is something called Transforming Power, a concept that is hard to explain, but no one who has experienced it would doubt its existence. It is a power within us all, a creative capacity that, if we get ourselves out of the way and allow enough space and time, can bring forth a new solution, something not expected, neither this nor that but something else.

Quakers experience it too in their business meetings when the worshipping community allows enough time for silence, listening and letting go of entrenched positions to allow the Spirit to enter in. The experience is akin to the holding of paradox that is so important in Eastern religions and was well understood by the mediaeval Christian mystic, Meister Eckhart.

We have seen that in all lives there is a measure of what the world might call success and failure, and it's something that we might recognise in ourselves. It seems that human beings in general only view things in terms of their opposite. By holding the extremes of "success" and "failure" in balance, however, it might be possible to move into another dimension:

Opposites are abstract concepts belonging to the world of thought, and as such they are relative. By the very act of focusing our attention on any one concept we create its opposite...Mystics transcend this realm of intellectual concepts, and in transcending it, they become aware of the relativity and polar relationships of all opposites. They realize that good and bad, pleasure and pain, life and death, are not absolute experiences belonging to different categories, but are merely two sides of reality; extreme parts of a single whole... Since all opposites are interdependent, their conflict can never result in the total victory of one side, but will always be an interplay between the two sides... This notion of dynamic balance is essential to the way the unity of opposites is experienced in Eastern mysticism. It is never a static identity, but always a dynamic interplay between the two extremes. (Capra, 157-8)

The concept of the union of opposites is not peculiar to Eastern mysticism. It was central to the thought of both the Greek philosopher, Heraclitus, in the 6th Century BC and the German eighteenth-century philosopher, Hegel, as well as mystics from the Jewish tradition of the Kabbalah, and within Christianity.

Every actual thing involves a coexistence of opposed elements. Consequently to know, or, in other words, to comprehend an object is equivalent to being conscious of it as a concrete unity of opposed determinations. (Hegel's *Logic*, Par. 48, Zusatz 1).

For the principal point of divine completeness is that... in every thing is its opposite, and... that all its power truly comes from the opposing power
(RabbiDov Baer, Ner Mitzvah ve-Torah).

As we hold opposites together in paradoxical unity, knowing that both co-exist, we may go beyond the duality of opposites to an understanding of essential unity.

> If the Eye of the Heart were fully open and we had attained complete Divine Knowledge, we would see that these contraries are all resolved finally in an all-embracing *unity*: God and Man, pleasure and pain, success and failure are ultimately all one in God. But one can only reach this perception in and through the tension of opposites. (Smith, 26)

In such a state, notions of success and failure dissolve. Such concepts are, after all, about having an agenda, and can only exist from a judgemental and ego-centred position.

> The mystic knows of another dimension, one that cannot be measured, one that cannot be subordinated to will and intentions; one that we cannot be in charge of. It is a dimension that is not divided into subjects and objects, for all is one in it. It is a totally interconnected world. The mystic knows of something beyond the rational… It is a knowing that permeates all of life; a knowing that is not greedy, not wanting to prove anything. (Jarman, 10)

The nearer one is to that unitive dimension, the less there can be of the kind of separation that measures success. There is less division, less objectivising of another. The work in hand is about connectedness.

In Christianity, worshippers are expected to examine themselves; in the Roman Catholic church, confession serves as a vehicle for repentance (admitting spiritual failure, a falling short) and for absolution. The Examen (Examination of Consciousness) is a key part of the discipline of the Jesuits, and a form of inner evaluation. Ignatius gives five steps: Praise and Thanksgiving, Petition for Light, Examination of Conscience, Expression of Sorrow and Repentance, and Resolution to be more faithful to God (a personal internalisation of the Eucharist). Simpler adaptations include questions such as Where have I met and co-operated with the Spirit today? Where have I met and evaded the Spirit today? How do I speak to God about this? Or Where was Love today? How did I miss it? Meet it? The problem with such an exercise is that it is hard not to get stuck in either self-congratulation or guilt. The important part of any such spiritual process is make an acknowledgement and to move on. I have found a more constructive exercise to be to acknowledge the blessings of the day: to find three things, perhaps, for which I am grateful.

In a religious life, how would one measure success? A glimpse of the Divine, a day lived in the Presence? But the moment a consciousness of "well done" enters in, the sense has gone, the ego takes over, blocking the inner space that can be the home of the Spirit. Angela Ashwin likens the experience of prayer to time spent with a lover – not to get anything out of it, but just for the sake of it. Whether the experience leaves a positive glow or a feeling of emptiness, "the language of success and failure is meaningless here... What matters is that we stay there" (26).

What do we mean by success, anyway, when we know that nothing is achieved except through grace? Not I, but God in me.

I know for myself that we cannot own (in the sense of possessing) the results of our actions; we cannot take credit for an action that has come from our deep selves and that may well have been beneficial for someone. If there was a blessing on our action, we can only give thanks. We have a responsibility for the way we do something; if our intention was pure and in right ordering, we don't have responsibility for the result. (Jarman, 24)

What about failure? Oh, then, the dreaded word "sin" enters into the equation. Are we born with original sin? Or, to use the title of a book by Matthew Fox, Original Blessing? Original sin is such a damning, depressing and pessimistic concept. The Litany, or General Supplication, from the Church of England Book of Common Prayer repeats the phrase, "have mercy upon us miserable sinners" again and again, and begs God to deliver us from a whole catalogue of misbehaviour and misfortune:

> From all evil and mischief; from sin, from the crafts and assaults of the devil; from thy wrath, and from everlasting damnation, from all blindness of heart; from pride, vain-glory, and hypocrisy; from envy, hatred, and malice, and all uncharitableness, from fornication, and all other deadly sin; and from all the deceits of the world, the flesh, and the devil, from sedition, privy conspiracy, and rebellion; from all false doctrine, heresy, and schism; from hardness of heart, and contempt of thy Word and Commandment

as well as from natural disasters, such as "lightning and tempest, plague, pestilence, and famine, and from battle and murder, and from sudden death". Is this helpful?

Fox posits that the concept of original sin is not biblical, that it originates only from Augustus in the 1st century AD. The literal meaning of sin, "missing the mark", is less judgemental than the connotations it has acquired. Lucinda Vardey explains well the ongoing experience of finding the "mark":

> Sin is a term used in archery for missing the mark, the bull's eye. The mark, the central point of our souls, takes some practice getting to. Freedom isn't something that just arrives one morning: it takes some chipping at the hard stones of our attitudes, thoughts, conditioning and egos. As if a paradox, the doorway to freedom is through obedience to the call of

God and a commitment to God's will over ours. (www.dallaluce.com)

And in many traditions, from Eckhart to Buddhism, the sin behind sin is that of dualism: treating another as an object outside oneself.

Gandhi held to the Buddhist and Jain view that all sins are modifications of *himsa*, that the basic sin, the only sin in the ultimate analysis, is the sin of separateness, or *attavada*. According to a Jain maxim, he who conquers this sin, conquers all others. (Rhagavan Iyer, quoted in Fox, 49)

We all know we fall short, miss the mark, at every turn. Failure is a minute-by-minute occurrence, if we choose to see it that way. Acknowledgement – even confession – can be healthy, but the important thing is to recognise our human fallibility – and be kind to ourselves. We know we are not perfect; we also know that we have strengths and talents. As the Unitarians/Unity Church put it:

We are created to be "healthy, happy, prosperous, loved and loving, courageous and strong". If we fall short of these goals, it is because we have separated our mind from God, and allowed negative thoughts to intrude. God is within each one of us; and is directly accessible. We need only to quietly turn within ourselves to contact God. (www.bible.ca/cr-Unity.htm)

From this positive viewpoint, we can acknowledge our gifts, as things given. It is not false pride to acknowledge them: we can hardly pat ourselves on the back for qualities we have been born with. Acknowledge them, see them as opportunities – and move on. One of the important balancing acts in the spiritual life is that between humility and the proper expression of our gifts. This is an important subject for Father James: "Quite a lot of a priest's ministry is how we manage our time – how I can be of most service – so it's important to think about what one can best contribute."

This way of life is not about relying on personal credit or external rewards. Buddhism, for instance, calls on us not to be attached the fruits of our labours. Peace-worker Roswitha Jarman has written of the way in which she approaches her work:

It has been important for me in my peace work not to come with expectations or looking for acknowledgement or praise for what I have done. The important thing was to do the tasks that were put in my way with inner commitment and, as Woolman would say, knowing that "Love was the first motion". Ultimately, we cannot know the effect our work has; if there are positive results, they are not for us to own, they belong to the source from which our love and compassion arose. The same applies to unsuccessful interventions. We are only responsible for the manner in which we executed the task, and in the way we were present to the task, we are not responsible for the result. It is the way we live and in the way our lives have touched the lives of others that the fruits of our actions lie. (Jarman, 23-4)

There is another approach to life, less goal-directed, more mindful, with the focus on the way, the process, living with intention and love. If the process is open and there is no outcome in mind, where is the success or failure? We need to let go of the burden of expectation and the pressure to achieve. Then we can do things without a "why". Do them in purity, because it is right. Mother Teresa is quoted as saying, "God has not called me to be successful; he has called me to be faithful."

What matters is living our lives in the power of love and not worrying too much about the results. In doing this, the means become part of the end. Hence we lose the sense of helplessness and futility in the face of the world's crushing problems. We also lose the craving for success, always focusing on the goal to the exclusion of the way of getting there. We must literally not take too much thought for the morrow but throw ourselves whole-heartedly into the present. That is the beauty of the way of love; it cannot be planned and its end cannot be foretold. (Wolf Mendl, 1974. *Quaker Faith & Practice*, 24.60)

When we are engaged in something, when all that matters is the work in hand, the relationship with the individual in front of us, concepts of success and failure simply don't exist. Since his experience of being sent to prison for something he didn't do, Joseph is in a different place: "The more I thought about success and failure, the more I realised that the things I used to think of as failures weren't. I just don't think like that any more." On his death bed? He can't imagine looking back. "What has the past to do with how I am now? That's what I focus on. What importance does it have? If you're at peace inside you, anything is possible. It's how you treat the moment."

When I asked Paule what her first reaction had been to my asking to talk to her about success and failure, she said, "I couldn't imagine that I would have anything to say. If you'd asked me ten or even five years ago, I'd have had some quite ordinary answers."

The concept doesn't exist for you?

"Something like that."

Irrelevant?

"Yes, though it's not irrelevant in the world; for people in general it's a huge matter. A few years ago I would have thought; what would I like to be successful. Now all I can do is wonder what would it be for success in the world."

And what do you think?

"A hope and a belief that one day there will be a change of consciousness in humans. That's the only way things can change. Though it's highly possible that the world has what it needs at the moment."

And, on your deathbed?

About twenty years ago, I thought that I was dying. From first going to the doctor to the end result of "it's OK" was a month. I lived that month knowing I was going to die. Things I had thought I wanted to do before I died were meaningless. I lived in great peace, in bliss. Words came to me: "I've come from the earth, and I'm going back to the earth." There was no clear meaning, just a sense of return.

Hubert feels that the change of consciousness is already happening, in each one of us. It can't be planned, but the power of our collective changing may, he feels, have a considerable impact on the future of the world.

It is hard to escape habitual ways of thinking. Even in our spiritual lives there seems to be an assumption that we are heading somewhere: we are, it seems, on a path, on a journey. From where to where? From A to B? Where do we expect to arrive? Heaven, Nirvana, Enlightenment? A place of complete understanding, when all doubt will fall away? Or is our aim to have peak experiences, to live in some heightened state of ecstasy? The history of experience in many faiths is that such states are in general transitory, and do not in any case form the bread and butter of the religious life. There is no ladder of hierarchy in the life of the Spirit. More to the point is a life devoted to love and service, a life such as that of a seventeenth-century French lay brother called Brother Lawrence. In his classic work of the spiritual life, *The Practice of the Presence of God*, he explains his life's practice in which he simply did everything – mainly washing up in the monastery kitchen – for the love of God. As Jennifer Rees Larcombe says in her preface to his book, if judged by the criteria of the world, he would have been a natural member of her childhood Failures Club.

A traditional view of prayer is to ask something of God. In petitionary or supplicatory prayer we pray *for* things, that they may happen; there is an expectation of an outcome. But what is the right outcome? Who are we to think that we know it? We pray that our wishes be fulfilled. But how do we know what to wish for? Hard as it may be, our current suffering may be just what is needed for spiritual growth. Prayer of this kind is still making assumptions about our own knowledge; we are still trying to be in control. But Angela Ashwin's approach is different: "When we pray, our aim is to be transparent to God, not to get God to be obedient to us" (29).

Or, as Trappist monk Thomas Merton, puts it:

We were indoctrinated so much into means and ends that we don't realise that there is a different dimension in the life of prayer. In technology you have this horizontal progress, where you must start at one point and move to another and then another. But that is not the way to build a life of prayer. In prayer we discover what we already have. You start where you are and you deepen what you already have. And you realise that you are already there. (From *Seeds of Contemplation*, Quoted on http://www.gratefulness.org/ readings/dsr_merton_recol.htm)

This view of spiritual growth may be described not as a journey but as a deepening, a flowering: the exquisite blossoming of a lotus flower. And, as a friend commented, "It is rooted in mud"!

We have heard earlier about how the unforeseen can intervene in the best of plans. If we let go of plans, we are giving the unforeseen more of a chance. In our creative selves, the part of us that goes beyond the routine certainties of everyday life, it is spontaneity, being open to the unexpected, that matters. If we recognise that it is the unforeseen that might have the most importance in our lives, we may allow ourselves to welcome uncertainty. Anxiety or worry about outcomes is not only pointless, it is a symptom of a lack of trust. Brother Lawrence didn't even prepare for tasks, just entrusted them to God, and he knew that all would be well. Julian of Norwich too knew in the core of her being that "all shall be well. All manner of things shall be well." But belief of this kind is not some starry eyed Pollyanna-ish naïveté but in both people was grounded in an inner peace developed over years of experience, struggle and suffering.

As we move into the realm of the heart and open it, that is, as we saw in Chapter 7, to allow ourselves to be vulnerable. In so doing we also open ourselves to the possibility of a different kind of knowing. If we set aside our rational priorities, and trust our experience and inner rather than outward certainty, we may find a kind of knowing that has a different, intuitive, quality. A different kind of knowledge, not limited to facts and practicalities based on the senses, or information derived from the senses, but knowing with the entire being. Then, rather than being frustrated by the things we do not know or understand, we will realise that there is much that we cannot rationally know, and find contentment in that unknowing. In this fallow ground of darkness germinate the seeds of our spiritual growth and creative selves. In living through times of dryness and doubt we are putting our trust in a process that we can never fully understand. Then we can discover the joy, as the twentieth-century American Quaker, Thomas Kelly, puts it, of "walking with a smile into the dark". Speaking on "Wonders of the Universe" on BBC television, Professor Brian Cox said, "That is the most beautiful place for a scientist to be: on the borders of the known and the unknown."

For the mystic, too, that is true.

If we let go of our judgemental behaviour, we will no longer view life in terms of success or failure.

If we let go of the need to know or control our lives, we will let go of goals and expectation.

If we let go of our attachment to outcomes, we will be content with where and who we are.

Further reading

Ashwin, Angela, *Faith in the Fool*. London: Darton, Longman and Todd, 2010

The *Bhagavad Gita*, trans. Juan Mascaro. New Delhi: Penguin Classics, 2009

Boyce, Frank Cottrell: "The joys of failure". BBC Radio 3, Free Thinking lecture, 9.12.10

Capra, Fritjof, *The Tao of Physics*. London: third edition, Flamingo, 1982

Harford, Tim, *Adapt: Why Success Always Starts with Failure*. London: Little, Brown, 2011

Hillson, David (ed.), *The Failure Files*. Devon: Triarchy Press, 2011

Jarman, Roswitha, *Breakthrough to Unity*. London: The Kindlers, 2010

Kohn, Alfie, *No Contest*. Boston, MA: Houghton Mifflin, 1993

Kohn, Alfie, *Punished by Rewards: The Trouble with Gold Stars, Incentive Plans, A's, Praise and Other Bribes*. Boston, MA: Houghton Mifflin, 2000

Leat, Diana, *Just Change; strategies for increasing philanthropic impact*. London: Association of Charitable Foundations, 2007

Rosenberg, Marshall, *Nonviolent Communication: a language of life*. Encinitas, California: Puddledancer Press, 2003

Schulz, Kathryn, *Being Wrong: Adventures in the Margin of Error*. London: Portobello Books, 2010

Smith, Cyprian, *The Way of Paradox*. London: Darton, Longman and Todd, 1987

Townsend, Mark, *The Gospel of Falling Down*. Ropley, Hants: O Books, 2007

Tzu, Lao, *Tao Te Ching*, translated with an introduction by D.C. Lao. London: Penguin, 1969

Walshe, Neale Donald, *Communion with God*. London: Hodder & Stoughton, 2000

BOOKS

O is a symbol of the world, of oneness and unity. In different cultures it also means the "eye," symbolizing knowledge and insight. We aim to publish books that are accessible, constructive and that challenge accepted opinion, both that of academia and the "moral majority."

Our books are available in all good English language bookstores worldwide. If you don't see the book on the shelves ask the bookstore to order it for you, quoting the ISBN number and title. Alternatively you can order online (all major online retail sites carry our titles) or contact the distributor in the relevant country, listed on the copyright page.

See our website **www.o-books.net** for a full list of over 500 titles, growing by 100 a year.

And tune in to myspiritradio.com for our book review radio show, hosted by June-Elleni Laine, where you can listen to the authors discussing their books.

MySpiritRadio